LIMERICKS

ISAAC ASIMOV

AND

JOHN CIARDI

Gramercy Books
New York

This 2000 edition is published by Gramercy Books™, an imprint of Random House Value Publishing, Inc. 201 East 50th Street, New York, N.Y. 10022 by arrangement with W. W. Norton & Company, Inc., New York.

Gramercy Books™ and design are trademarks of Random House Value Publishing, Inc.

Random House
New York • Toronto • London • Sydney • Auckland
http://www.randomhouse.com/

Library of Congress Cataloging–in–Publication Data

Asimov, Isaac, 1920-1992
  [Limericks, too gross]
  Limericks / Isaac Asimov and John Ciardi.
      p. cm.
  Previously published as two separate works: Limericks, too gross (1978) and Grossery of limericks (1981).
  ISBN 0-517-20882-2
  1. Limericks. I. Ciardi, John, 1916- II. Asimov, Isaac, 1920- Grossery of limericks. III. Title.

PS3551.S5 L45 2000
811'.07508—dc21

                                                                        99-058756

Printed and bound in the United States of America.

9 8 7 6 5 4 3 2 1

Contents

To John
    I hope I didn't make you look too bad
            —Isaac

To Isaac
    Eat your heart out
            —John

Dedicated to all the chairmen (and other drunks) of all the
English Departments I ever roared out a Saturday night with—
and to all genial lechers, wherever met.
            —John

Foreword I
by John Ciardi

*   *   *

Isaac Asimov and the Art of the Limerick

There is some bond between limerick and the English language that seems as natural as the bond between a clam and a sandy sea bottom, as if one had been specifically fitted to the other by the long tunings of evolution. Yet the limerick is a relatively recent form, and probably not even native to English. The first known specimens date from the early eighteenth century, and they are in French.

The Irish Brigade served in France from 1691 to about

1780. Its officers may have imported the form to Limerick in Ireland, whence the name of the form. Alternatively, the name may derive from the carousers' refrain "Will you come up to Limerick?" This refrain was once sung in chorus by the assembled drunkards after one among them had sung a solo verse. The solo need not have been a limerick as we know it. Perhaps it was sung to a roughly similar form. Perhaps it was even common at one time to sing limericks. Or perhaps not. Everything about the origin of the limerick—like Isaac Asimov's metric—is just a touch uncertain.

Yet one thing is sure. The form has survived many curious impositions in its brief history, and it will survive Isaac's. I have appended my own gross of limericks to this collection primarily to show that the form is not dead, though any reader who starts at the beginning of this book will find cause enough to fear for the limerick's life.

Like most growing things, the limerick had to suffer an age of innocence. It was Edward Lear (1812–1888) who tuned it to sweet nonsense, though usually with a hobbled last line in the manner of:

> There was a young man of Quebec
> Who stood in snow up to his neck.
>   When asked, "Ain't you friz?"
>   He replied, "Yes, I is.
> But we don't call this cold in Quebec."

Neither do we call it a limerick today. The true form absolutely demands that third rhyme, and (as I have tried to explain to a high-speed typist named Isaac who plays incessant literary chopsticks on three IBM Selectrics at once) what it demands is that the rhyme be both deft and outrageous. This typist has never found it hard to be outrageous. Unfortunately, he learned his deftness by rule of thumbs— ten of them.

It is for that reason that I have just sent him to the blackboard to copy out the following classic limerick fifty times, wiping the slate clean between each careful copy. As an exception to his fixed rule, I have insisted that he take time to think about what he is writing. No one who writes as he does can take time to think, and I am afraid my insistence may slow him down, but he will learn that I mean only to improve his writing habits. Here is the limerick:

> There was a young lady from Chichester
> Whose beauty made saints in their niches stir.
>> One morning at matins
>> Her breast in rose satins
> Made the bishop of Chichester's britches stir.

Alternatively, he may write the last rhyme as *brichester*.

. . . Go ahead, Isaac. I will be speaking to these nice people while you keep usefully busy. . . .

Something in the tutelary spirit of the limerick soon took it from Lear to leer. It can still romp among the innocent, but it is naturally drawn to rolling about with the satyrs, or among the satyric fantasies of the drunken.

So it was that Victorian and post-Victorian Britains of donnish tastes, suffering from the great gray queen's plague of inhibitions, seized upon the limerick as a more or less sanctioned way of venting all the four-letter words they had stored up as schoolboys. I suspect, though I cannot prove, that limericks of this sort tend to be British. The following specimen is certainly British:

> On the bank sat the bishop of Buckingham.
> He was cooling his balls—he was ducking 'em.
> > While observing the stunts
> > Of the cunts in the punts
> And the tricks of the pricks as was fucking 'em.

And certainly this one:

> Said the dowager duchess at tea,
> "Young man, do you fart when you pee?"
> > I replied, "Not a bit.
> > Do you belch when you shit?"
> —Which I'd say left the honours with me.

The following limerick, on the other hand—with "cold comfort" as one of the choicest locutions in the whole range of English poetry—cannot fail to be American:

> Said a widow whose singular vice
> Was to keep her dead husband on ice,
>   "It's been hard since I lost him.
>   I'll never defrost him.
> Cold comfort, but cheap at the price."

Let me say within hearing of that person at the blackboard, gentle readers, that I have no thought of taking all Americans to be subtle wits, nor of taking all Britains to be four-letter scalawags. I have known several Britains who were as approximately witty as science-fiction writers. Nor can one afford to be randomly snobbish, especially one who collaborates as indiscriminately as I do.

Whether or not the distinction is national, there is the limerick (and it can be very good) that serves mostly as an outlet for all the no-no words, and there is, on the other hand, the limerick honed to the subtleties of "single entendre."

One or the other, or both at once, the limerick naturally turns into a *roman à cleft*, and in the twentieth century its most natural habitat in America has been the Saturday night faculty swozzle led by the sots of the English Department.

The limerick has become a passion of academic drunkards to such an extent that even a fat ex-biochemist retooled as a universal genius has dared offer himself as a limericker— and without even the excuse of being an alcoholic. He is in fact a teetotaler.

Somewhere beyond the last space warp, where the ultimate parsec starts to curve back from beyond time, I shall have to stand before my tribal gods and explain to them how I came to associate with a teetotaler. I may then argue that the fellow's behavior is so naturally besotted that one tends to think of him as a drunkard, though the spirit is not in him. In better conscience, I could certainly argue that I have drunk enough for any two and that I have sought to assign my excess of merit to him, for it is only natural that such hack writers seek increase in association with the more spiritedly literate. And I shall infallibly point out as his saving graces, first, that he is a dirty old man, and second, that he has renounced academe. For reasons known only to his own hard-clutched psyche, he has insisted on retaining the title of his tenure, and is still an in-name-only Associate Professor of Biochemistry at Boston University, which can no longer bid for his services against the rates now available to selected speed-typists who manage to persuade editors that such typing is an act of genius.

I shall, finally, plead long friendship. We are both native Bostonians. I knew him when even he wasn't entirely sure he was a genius. I have grown to depend upon him as the penitential soul depends upon its hair shirt. Any one hour in the wind tunnel of this man's wit, I am persuaded, will release me from a century of future purgatorial pain—if I am not dragged beyond salvation by ill-chosen companions.

As a test of my piety and forebearance, I have even forced myself to endure his pretensions to the ministry of the True Limerick. I will not go so far as to say he has profaned it. It would be more accurate to say he has propaned it. Or dieseled it. Hell, I think, will turn out to be diesel-powered. Isaac has obviously been having a hell of a time with the limerick, for once he is through grinding its gears, it never fails to give off the attar of a New York City bus on a muggy day.

The limerick—as I hope he may yet learn by consulting the truly written second half of this book—is a subtler and less noisy thing. I am not entirely convinced the art of it is entirely beyond him. Given such example, I don't see why even he could not learn. For he is conscientious. His work at the blackboard, for instance, has been. . . .

But why is he adding all those footnotes? Just look at what he has done:

Chichester. Earlier *Cisseceaster.* The second element, *chester,* derives from Latin *castra,* fortified place. The first element is probably from *Cissa*, also known as *Cissi*, son of Aelli (whoever he was). Note that with Old English "c" sounded as a kappa, the original name was pronounced approximately "kissy keester"—a delicious subtlety, for though only the young lady's breasts are overtly stated to have enflamed His Worship, the very place name, with all the delicacy and force of a subliminal suggestion, introduces her *kissy keester* as a further source of the bishop's lay impulse.

What drivel! I can only suppose he has been reading some of those heavy-handed collections in which the limerick is reduced to little more than a vehicle for arch footnotes. Was it Norman Douglas ("South Wind" Douglas) who started this fashion? His early under-the-counter collection smothered the limerick in such stuff in much the way the local greasy spoon smothers liver with onions, to disguise a questionable taste. Or is it only that the limerick has been taken over by academics who have brought to it their habit of living as footnotes to their own psyches? It won't do. Excuse me. I must put an end to this once and . . .

—*No, Isaac. The first commandment is: Thou shalt not commit felonious footnotery. Come now, there is no need to sulk. Yes, alas, I love you. But is it love if everything must be explained in footnotes? Erase them, I say.*

—*There. See for yourself how nicely it does without such stuff.*

—*Of course, I have faith in you. Once you have learned to read, there is no end to what you might not overachieve. Yes, I know you have been so busy writing that you haven't had time to become literate. But just take things one at a time. And the first thing to learn about the limerick is that it must stand on its own or it just can't stand.*

Why don't you start by reading to me what you have written on the blackboard? —Sorry. I forgot you can't read. What? You'll write me a limerick instead? A whole gross of them? Oh, I see: you want me to turn the page and read what you have written so you can hear how it sounds. Suppose I skip to the back of the book and read some real limericks to you? You'd rather hear your own. Well, why not? I, too, was a professor once—a Full Professor, of course—and I always took pleasure in the challenge offered by what used to be called the "unusual" student.

You point to the words, and I will say them for you. But first, please excuse me, while I apologize to what readers you haven't frightened away. You turn the page and find the place. I'll be right with you.

. . . Sorry, dear reader. Please forgive the interruption. I shall be delighted to have you join our reading, if you care to stay. But let me beg you to understand about Isaac. He is a self-made man and a remarkable one. He has, in fact, some remark or other on every known subject, and on several unknown ones. But being self-made is a bit like turning out your own picture frames. They come out square enough, and they look fine from a distance, but once you come close enough to examine the miters, you understand how much difference a touch of professionalism could have made.

To change metaphors, since we are inviting you to some sort of feast, I am afraid the wine you will be starting with won't qualify as a true vintage. Yet it is a zesty little wine, ordinary but pert, and pleasantly brash in its own way. At least try it.

Once it is out of the way, I can promise you your choice of a dozen dozen from Bacchus's own cellar.

Chin-chin,

John Ciardi
Bill Nimmo's Bar
Metuchen, N.J.

Foreword II
by Isaac Asimov

John Ciardi and the Art of the Foreword

There are those (John Ciardi among them) who say that John Ciardi has written children's poetry that can't be better; that he has done a translation of Dante that all but improves on the original; that he has a voice that can read even the telephone book and make it sound beautiful; but I—

I have always held John Ciardi to be the very model of behavior and the pink of deportment. All should behold the man and observe him narrowly, for whatever he does, why do the contrary and you will be *right*.

Some people fall short of perfection most of the time, but John Ciardi never does. Without fail, without exception, without swerving to either right or left a hair's-breadth, he invariably does the perfectly wrong thing.

With all that in mind, I read his Foreword, the same one you have just skipped. Since he was long, verbose, and muddy, I shall be brief, terse, and luminously clear. Since he was heavy-handed and quoted filthy limericks he did not write, I will be deft and quote clean limericks that I did write. I shall quote three of them, in fact, and all about John Ciardi:

1. To make friends with the lumpish John Ciardi
   Needs a spirit uncouth, rough, and hardy.
   > When in line for a bit
   > Of amusement and wit—
   Did he get it? Why, no, he was tardy.

2. To a dinner arrived fat John Ciardi
   With only his appetite hearty.
   > Conversational ploys?
   > He had nothing but noise,
   And he spoiled every bit of the party.

3. What more shall I say of John Ciardi?
   His humor is junk, his wit shoddy.
       To speak of his mind
       Would be most unkind
   And, God, would you look at that body.

There you are, John. It took you many pages to decide you had finally managed to deflate me. The job of deflating you is far easier.

Isaac Asimov

Limericks: A Gross by Isaac Asimov

1. POLITENESS

Breathed a tender young man from Australia,
"My darling, please let me unveilia,
  And then, oh, my own,
  If you'll kindly lie prone,
I'll endeavor, my sweet, to impalia.

2. DUCKBILL PLATYPUS

"We refuse," said two men from Australia,
"Bestiality this saturnalia.
  For now, we bethink us,
  The ornithorhynchus
Is our down-under type of Mammalia."

3. EDWARDIAN

Lady Gwendolyn, skirts all a-rustle,
Resisted and put up a tussle,
  But the wicked old earl
  With his fingers a-curl
At last managed a pinch on the bustle.

4. A MERE TRIFLE

Said a certain young man with a grin,
"I think it is time to begin."
    Said the girl with a sneer,
    "With what? Why, your pee-er
Is scarcely as big as a pin."

5. WITH MEAT SAUCE

There was a young woman named Betty
Who thought waterbeds rather petty.
    The results were less hasty,
    She thought, and more tasty,
If one screwed on a bed of spaghetti.

6. APOSTATE

There once was a daring young Jew
Who said to his rabbi, "Screw you,
    I eat meat on Yom Kippur
    Mixed with milk by the dipper,
And as for the shiksehs—woo, woo!"

7. SHE KNOWS WHAT SHE WANTS

There was a young woman of Essex
Who had many occasions to bless sex
    And would banish from sight
    Any moron who might
Suggest it was time she had less sex.

8. ONLY NATURAL

A young nun from Long Beach, California,
Said, "I think it's important to warnia
    That though seeming a saint
    I've an awful complaint,
I am just getting steadily hornia."

9. BIG MOUTH

Said young Joseph to beautiful Nadya,
"It's many long years since I hadya."
    Said she, "You're a rat
    To talk about that.
Why can't you keep secrets, you cadya?"

10. BIOLOGY

Said an ovum one night to a sperm,
"You're a very attractive young germ.
    Come join me, my sweet,
    Let our nuclei meet
And in nine months we'll both come to term."

11. THE HORRORS OF DRINK

When a certain young woman named Terry
Got drunk on a small sip of sherry
    She'd insist upon games
    With embarrassing names
Not in any refined dictionary.

12. THERE SHE GOES

There is a young lass of Valencia
For whom sex is a form of dementia.
    For the first hour she's quiet
    Then she builds to a riot
With a noise that grows quickly intensia.

13. SEEK AND YE SHALL FIND

Said a certain young girl of Madrid
Who kept her vagina well hid,
    "For a lousy peseta,
    I am no fornicata,
But I'll spread for an adequate bid."

14. TIME INDEED

"It is time," said a woman from Devon,
"To exchange maiden bliss for sex heaven.
    There is music, it's spring,
    Flowers bloom, birdies sing;
And besides I've just turned thirty-seven."

15. FRIGID

There's a beautiful woman named Pam
Whose sexy appearance is sham
    When a man wants a lay
    She yawns and says, "Nay!"
And he stands there frustrated. God damn!

16. IT'S TRUE

There's a certain young woman named Janet
Who's the sexiest dish on the planet.
    From her toe to her palm
    She's a nuclear bomb
And no one, thank God, wants to ban it.

17. MUSICAL CHAIRS

There was a young fellow named Hal
Whose wife ran away with his pal.
    He abhorred deprivation
    So he found consolation
In the arms of another friend's gal.

18. PRIDE

At a nudist camp, sweet little Lillian
Was slated to lead the cotillion.
    This made her so proud
    That to shine in the crowd
She painted her nipples vermilion.

19. GRAMMAR

"Adultery," said Joseph, "is nice.
If once is all right, better twice.
        This doubling of rations
        Improves my sensations
For the plural of spouse, friend, is spice."

20. TOO FAT

Said a woman from Richmond, Virginia,
"I'd be rich if I only were skinnia.
        If I lost thirty pounds
        The boys would have grounds
To say, 'How I'd pay to be inia.' "

21. OH, YEAH?

A prim Texan, when caught in sin's vortex,
Would mutter, "Let go of that whore, Tex.
        You must never employ her
        You don't really enjoy her
All that pleasure is just in your cortex."

22.   NOTHING TO IT

A young woman, polite and demure,
Would reform the depraved and impure.
　　She found it a breeze
　　And did it with ease
For her work was a mere sinecure.

23.   FRUSTRATION

There was an old fellow from Anchorage
Who was riddled with fury and rancorage.
　　When he offered abusement
　　The girls gave refusement
And all he was left with was hankerage.

24.   SEA DOG

A captain, exposed to alarms
And much given to shivers and qualms,
　　Just couldn't keep warm
　　On a boat in a storm
Without the first mate in his arms.

25. REALISM

There was a young fellow named Clark
Who decided that sex was a lark.
        Since he couldn't endure
        The sight of a whore
He would always make love in the dark.

26. HOW NICE

Said a guy to his gal, quite ambitiously,
"I will screw you, my dear, expeditiously."
        The lass simply smiled,
        Said, "Delightful! Just wild!"
And it all ended simply deliciously.

27. RIGHT, LEFT, RIGHT, LEFT

There was a young woman from Venice
Who's a regular sexual menace.
        She would hop from one boy
        To another, with joy,
Like a ball in a fast game of tennis.

28. ECONOMY

There's a man who is named Isidore
Who has never made love to a whore.
    It is not that he frowns
      At the ups and the downs;
He just thinks paying cash is a bore.

29. WHAT'S YOUR HURRY?

A certain young man was so deft
That he left his poor girl quite bereft.
    He'd put it in slickly
      Then pull it out quickly
And before she had felt it, he'd left.

30. MAY I HAVE THE HONOR?

There was a young woman named Suzie
Who was not much inclined to be choosy
    So that after a day
      Of intensive sex play
She was apt to remark, "Say, just who's he?"

31. IF

My boy, if you like to have fun,
If you take all the girls one by one,
      And when reaching four score
      Still don't find it a bore,
Why, then, you're a hero, my son.

32. MODERATION

There was an old fellow named Reese
Who longed to make love to his niece.
      Don't accuse him of gall,
      He did not expect all,
But just an occasional piece.

33. JUST POSSIBLY

Said a very attractive young Haitian,
"Please begin with a gentle palpation.
      If you do as I say
      In the way of sex play
Why, who knows, there may be fornication."

34. AIM LOW

A young fellow, with rueful veracity,
Said he hadn't much phallic capacity;
    So he tried no one new
    Stayed with girls he could screw,
And that's what I call perspicacity.

35. WRONG PLACE, WRONG TIME

There was a young fellow named Ned
Who'd invent comic verses in bed.
    In the end the poor simp
    Let his penis grow limp
And the woman beneath bashed his head.

36. ACCIDENT

I got into bed with Dolores
And her diaphragm proved to be porous.
    The result of our sins
    Was a fine pair of twins;
Now the birth control people abhor us.

37. DISAPPOINTMENT

A certain young fellow named Scott
Once jumped his young bride on their cot.
 He intended no shirking
 But from sheer overworking
A dry run is all that she got.

38. WHY, SISTER!

A young nun who made notes in her diary
That were terribly torrid and fiery
 Once left it behind
 For her abbess to find.
Now she isn't allowed in the priory.

39. FIT FOR A MARATHON

To the ancient Greek writer, Herodotus,
Said a pretty young thing, "My, how hard it is."
 Said he, "Do you fear
 I will hurt you, my dear?"
And she said, "Are you crazy? Thank God it is."

40. HOW CUTE!

Said Jane, "I just love to exhibit,
A delight I let nothing inhibit.
    I think it's a ball
    To undress and bare all.
Oh, I'm such a young flibbertigibbet."

41. GELATINOUS

There wasn't a soul with a fatter ass
Than a maiden who lived at Cape Hatteras.
    When stroked it would wiggle
    And shiver and jiggle.
Men lined up, by the score, just to pat 'er ass.

42. MUTTER, MUTTER

There was a young woman named Shirley
With eyes blue and cheeks pink and teeth pearly.
    Her figure curved nicely
    Where it ought to precisely,
And when she said, "No," men grew surly.

43. TEMPORARY

There was a young lass named Theresa
Whom the fellows all longed for a piece o';
    But she isn't for sale
    To some lustful old male.
You can't buy 'er—but money will lease 'er.

44. UNFAIR COMPETITION

There was a young fellow named Sturgis
Who needed a lass for his urges,
    But how could he buy
    With the price bid sky-high
By the men of the various clergies?

45. DESPERATE

There's a certain young woman named Fran
Who has it whenever she can.
    But that's not really much
    So she's ripe for the touch
Of just any old warm-blooded man.

46. OH, DON'T TELL ME

A devout Jewish maiden named Donna
Is extremely afraid she's a goner.
    She was screwing one day
    In each possible way
Quite forgetting it was Rosh Hashana.

47. PRINCIPLES

There was once a remarkable stripper
Who'd undress to the very last zipper
    Before one—before all—
    But one day in the fall
She refused and said, "Not on Yom Kippur."

48. MIGHTY

There was a young fellow from Dallas
Who was rugged, enormous, and callous.
    He would shatter chrome steel
    With one blow of his heel
Then powder the bits with his phallus.

49. HOW GODLIKE

A man with a prick of obsidian,
Of a length that was truly ophidian,
    Was sufficiently gallant
    To please girls with his talent
Each day in the midpostmeridian.

50. IN ALPHABETICAL ORDER?

There was a young lover named Marius
Whose approaches to sex were quite various.
    He kept in his files
    All possible styles
That came under the head of nefarious.

51. HURRY!

At his wedding, a bridegroom named Crusoe
Was embarrassed to find his prick grew so.
    His eager young bride
    Pulled him quickly astride
And was screwed while still wearing her trousseau.

5 2 . SOFTER SIDE

The haughty philosopher, Plato,
Would unbend to a sweet young tomato.
    Though she might be naive
    Like you wouldn't believe
He would patiently show her the way to.

5 3 . CAUGHT!

Poor old John doesn't really do much;
Here and there just a fugitive touch.
    But his wife happened by
    When his palm stroked a thigh
Now the fellow is really in dutch.

5 4 . PEEK-A-BOO

The excitement produced by Miss Whipple
Was very much more than a ripple.
    She was covered with clothes
    From her head to her toes
Save for delicate holes at each nipple.

55. ZZZZ

> I'm afraid one can hardly suppose
> A presence as boring as Joe's.
> > When he's finally led
> > A girl into bed
> She promptly falls into a doze.

56. ANYTHING TO PLEASE

> Bill maintains that he isn't inclined
> To value a girl for her mind.
> > But to help him get in
> > He will do that and grin,
> Though he'd rather admire her behind.

57. DISAPPOINTMENT

> Said an angry young damsel, "What meanness!
> First a fellow will brag of his penis,
> > Then you say, 'Come on, lover,
> > Why don't you uncover?'
> And he does—and you're shocked at the wee-ness."

58. EITHER WAY

Said a certain young fellow from Texas,
"You can't dream how extremely it vexes
 My mother that I,
 However I try,
Stay attracted to both of the sexes."

59. THAT INDEFINABLE SOMETHING

"I'm falling in love with young Liz, ma!"
Said Johnny one morning to his ma.
 "Her breast size, you see
 Is 42-G
And that gives a woman charisma."

60. CHÀCUN A SON GOUT

Said a certain young maid of Tortuga,
"How I wish I could mate with a cougar.
 The sheer joy of the matching
 Would be worth all the scratching."
But her friends think she's clearly meshuggah.

61.   ALWAYS THE WAY

There once was a handsome young sheik
With a marvelous penile physique.
    Its length and its weight
    Made it seem really great
But he fell very short on technique.

62.   IDENTIFICATION

Last night, a blind date phoned Amelia
And said, "I will wear a camellia.
    If you need something more
    You'll be satisfied for
I'm the one who'll at once get familiar."

63.   OUCH!

There was once a young fellow named Nick,
Who was terribly proud of his prick.
    Without fear it would bend
    He would bounce on its end.
As he said, "It's my own pogostick."

64. THE AYES HAVE IT

There was a fair woman named Kate
Who would prove such an excellent date
    That each fellow would note
    (A unanimous vote)
That she wasn't just fair—she was great!

65. SLAVE OF DUTY

There once was a lazy young clerk
Who thought sex a great deal of work.
    But he said, "When I shove
    It's a labor of love,
And that sort of thing I can't shirk."

66. FIRST THINGS FIRST

There's a certain young woman named Sharon
Who's decided to marry a baron.
    At age eighty-four
    He can do it no more.
But he's rich—so she isn't despairin'.

67. NO LUCK

To her mother said sorrowful Dagmar,
"My social life's simply a drag, ma.
    Of my men, there are two
    Who don't know how to screw
And the third is just simply a fag, ma."

68. VILLAGE IDIOT

There was a young fellow named Wayne
Who's too dumb to come out of the rain.
    He has learned, more or less,
    How to lift a girl's dress
More than that is too much for his brain.

69. SHIFTING GEARS

There's a certain erotic old bum
Whom no one can think of as dumb.
    At the end of a bout
    When his prick is worn out
He shifts to the use of his thumb.

70. SECRETIVE

A certain young girl of Bel Air
Once carefully braided the hair
    All over her crotch
    Letting nobody watch,
And the fellows all thought it unfair.

71. WHAT A RELIEF!

Said Wilma, "Last week I believed
I had slipped and had somehow conceived.
    My prayers were a myriad,
    And I then got my period,
And now, for a while, I'm reprieved."

72. NOT HER FAULT

Have you heard the incredible news
About Linda, who's off on a cruise?
    She had sex on the coral
    In ways most immoral
But John puts the blame on the booze.

73. DON'T LOSE THAT VOICE

There's an outlaw out there by El Paso
Who once dodged the old sheriff's thrown lasso.
    It was aimed for his nuts
    So good luck to the klutz.
To this day he is still singing basso.

74. A BIG IMPROVEMENT

A girl who was from Brooklyn Heights
Looked quite mediocre in tights.
    There was much more approval
    When, upon their removal,
She revealed more spectacular sights.

75. YES, MOTHER

There was a young girl from Bordeaux
Whose mother said, "Always say no!"
    But the girl said "No," *after*
    The fun, when with laughter,
She'd screwed her good friend, Pierrot.

76. ADVANTAGE

There once was a young spaced-out drummer
Who, everyone said, was no bummer.
    He needs but one stick
    And that is his prick
And his pounding's what makes him a comer.

77. SO THEY GOT WET

There was a young woman named Ella
Who was caught in the rain with a fella,
    But were both so intent
    On complete ravishment
They forgot to put up an umbrella.

78. FAILURE

A dignified fellow named Cliff
Got into a hell of a tiff
    With his eager young wife
    In their newlywed life
When only his manner proved stiff.

79. HE'LL NEVER LEARN

There was an old fellow of Michigan
Who said, "Oh, I wish I were rich again,
    But each time I'm ahead
    I fall into the bed
Of that rotten old gold-digging bitch again."

80. I WONDER WHY

Said a certain young fellow from Utah,
"I've a girl, but I don't seem to suitah.
    I am tall; I am wise;
    I've got lovely blue eyes;
And in matters of sex I am neutah."

81. ENUNCIATION

An elderly sage of B'nai B'rith
Told his friend he was quite full of pith.
    This could mean "full of fact"
    And "with meaning compact,"
But not when you're lithping like thith.

8 2 . TOO BAD

As a poet, a young man named Buck
Was utterly lacking in luck.
> He tried limericks (lecherous)
> But found rhyming quite treacherous
And to rhyme "Buck" and "luck" left him stuck.

8 3 . GUESS WHAT!

To her lover said pretty young Julie,
"I don't want to alarm you unduly.
> I don't intend blame
> And yet, all the same,
You've produced a small pregnancy. —Truly!"

8 4 . READY!

There was a young lady named Lynne
Who said, "I'm prepared to begin
> Any sort of activity
> That suits my proclivity
Provided it counts as a sin."

85. GET WITH IT!

Said a certain young woman named Amy,
"I am seeking a fellow to tame me
    And teach me the newer
    Mad routes to l'amour
For to stay virgin longer will shame me."

86. LET'S NOT WATCH

There is a young woman named Rose
Who has a fixation on toes.
    She thinks that love's remedies
    Start with pedal extremities,
And she then passes on to—God knows!

87. YUM, YUM!

A gourmet's delight is Priscilla
For her breath's a distinct sarsparilla.
    One breast tastes of thyme
    The other of lime
And her vaginal flavor's vanilla.

88. DON'T CROWD

There was a young woman from Paris
Whom nothing at all could embarrass,
    So when screwing at night
    She would turn on the light
For the audience out on the terrace.

89. FOR A CHANGE

There was a young woman named Joan
Who once had six men of her own.
    The first was for Mondays
    Then the rest—except Sundays
When she'd just masturbate all alone.

90. ONLY FAIR

There was a young Frenchman, Marceau,
Who said to his girlfriend, "Ah, no.
    I admit it is sweet,
    Ma très chère petite,
But it's your turn to move down below."

91. WAITING FOR LEFTY

A young man, quite well known to be deft,
Said, "My dear, do not feel so bereft.
    Though I've sprained my right hand
    I'm not really unmanned.
I can diddle quite well with my left."

92. AW, SHUCKS

A voluptuous girl named Elaine
Greeted all Joe's attempts with disdain.
    When he took her to dinner
    And tried to get in 'er,
Where he only got "in" was "in vain."

93. SO STOP ALREADY

There was a young girl named Priscilla
With whom sex proved completely a thrilla
    One just can't get enough
    Of that girl's kind of stuff
(Although the sixth time it's a killa).

94. MR. AMERICA

How they marvel at Joe's penal vigor,
At its size and magnificent rigor.
    When he was a lad
    'Twas already not bad
And with age, it keeps on getting bigger.

95. SENSUAL PERCEPTION

There was a young man from Wilkes-Barre
Who, at following girls, was a star.
    His vision was poor,
    His hearing unsure,
But he sniffed pheromones from afar.

96. OH, APHRODITE

Said a chic and attractive young Greek,
"Would you like a quick peek that's unique?"
    "Why, yes," Joe confessed,
    So she quickly undressed
And showed him her sleek Greek physique.

97. WHY WASTE TIME?

Joe inspects girls with conscienceless suavity
In search of their luscious concavity,
    At which he will leap
    Like a wolf on a sheep
With utterly hardened depravity.

98. CAN'T TRUST THE BLOKE

While sleeping, a sailor from Twickenham
Was aware of a strange object stickenham.
    Before he could turn
    He'd occasion to learn
His shipmate was plunging his prickenham.

99. SAFETY FIRST

There once was a haughty old baronet
With a prick twice as long as a clarinet.
    If the thing ever dangled
    'Twould be stepped on and mangled,
So he kept it tucked inside a hair-i-net.

100. MODESTY

There was once an athletic young jock
Who could shatter large rocks with his cock,
    But a coed said, "Dear,
    Please insert the thing here."
And he fainted away with the shock.

101. CHOICE

Said Joe of a woman named Alison
"That's a lady with whom I would dally, son.
    For her body, you see,
    Is indubitably,
Where I'd like to deposit my phallus on."

102. ON TARGET

There was a young woman named Sally
Who loved an occasional dally.
    She sat on the lap
    Of a well-endowed chap
And said, "Ooo, you're right up my alley."

103. PRACTICAL

There was a young fellow named Si
Whose motto was "Never say die."
    Too plain to attract,
    He never attacked.
If he couldn't persuade, he would buy.

104. PLUG

A new volume of verse Asimovian
That's replete with a humor that Jovian
    Represents stimulation
    That will prove the occasion
For a laughing response quite Pavlovian.

105. DISAPPOINTMENT

There was a young woman name Jeannie
Who sobbed to her date, "You're a meanie.
    You claim you're a stud,
    But, oh, what a dud!
Your prick is a real teeny-weeny."

106. LUXURIANT

The dark pubic hair of young Sadie
Is the longest you'll find on a lady.
    You must guess at the angle
    When you push through that tangle,
But once there, the surroundings are shady.

107. MALFRAGRANCE

There was an old fellow named Eric
Whose breath made those near him choleric.
    He produced a hiatus,
    In crowds, with his flatus.
He's a one-man disease, atmospheric.

108. SKIN-DEEP

There's a woman whose name is Lucille
Who, whenever she chooses to peel,
    Discloses a skin
    One would love to get in
For the sake of its wonderful feel.

109. SECOND BEST, I'M AFRAID

Said Joe, "When I leave my young Stephanie
Her cries of unhappiness deafen me,
    But I make no apology,
    I rely on technology,
And screw her by wireless telephony."

110. SO DID BORIS GODUNOV

The eminent basso, Chaliapin,
Loved the sound of an audience clappin'.
    But that tuneful go-getter
    Loved one thing even better:
Spending few hours in bed simply nappin'.

111. NOT EASY

There was a young fellow named Paul
Whose prick was exceedingly small.
    When in bed with a lay
    He could screw her all day
Without touching the vaginal wall.

112. BITER BIT

Joe invited his girl to dutch treat,
Which sweetened the old balance sheet.
    Though he saved lots of dough,
    The next night proved a blow
When he could not arouse her to heat.

113. EASY GOING

A woman there was named Pauline
Who's always been terribly keen
    On kissing and wooing—
    Indiscriminate screwing—
And anything else that's obscene.

114. FALSE ADVERTISING

There was a young fellow named Barney
Who wanted to visit Killarney.
    He was told the colleens there
    Were screwing machines there
But found that was Irishmen's blarney.

115. GOOD FIT

"Near my girl," said a lecher named Cecil,
"Is the place where I usually nestle.
　　Nothing else is a patch
　　On the way that we match.
She's the mortar and I am the pestle."

116. WHAT A WASTE

There once was a woman named Baker,
A thoughtful and pious young Quaker.
　　She's terrifically stacked
　　But the tragical fact
Is that none of the fellows can make 'er.

117. DAYDREAM

Said a certain old lecher named Day,
"If my good wife would but go away,
　　I'd locate a young lass
　　And then let the world pass
And I'd do what comes natural and play."

118. GOOD THINKING

There was a fan-dancer of Cannes
Who developed an excellent plannes
　　For a lecherous dance
　　Without any pants
And some very big holes in the fannes.

119. YOU CAN'T HAVE
EVERYTHING

Daphne's looks are completely imperial
And her style of lovemaking's ethereal.
　　She's erotically active
　　And intensely attractive.
What a shame her disease is venereal!

120. SHOCKING

Comic verse of the type that's limerical
Prove to be, often times, anticlerical.
　　A saintly old minister
　　Is depicted as sinister
And as filled with a lust quite hysterical.

121. WATCH IT

There was an old fellow of Tripoli
Who used to make love rather nippily.
    Said his angry young lass
    While rubbing her ass,
"Less teethily, please, and more lippily."

122. VERSATILE

Shyly said a young woman named Mabel,
"How delighted I am that I'm able
    To screw on a bed
    —Or a sofa instead
—Or the grass—or the floor—or the table."

123. ELIZABETHAN

That old English stud, Walter Raleigh,
Was always remarkably jolly,
    Particularly
    When it happened that he
Was in bed with a buxom young dolly.

124. MONOTONOUS

Said a certain delightful old nut,
"I guess I am just in a rut
　　Made of breast and of lips
　　And vaginas and hips
And sometimes a well-rounded butt."

125. WOMEN'S LIB

A reporter who worked on the journal,
Once said to his girlfriend, "Why, sure, Nell,
　　If you don't mind a mess
　　Just hike up your dress
And then you can use a man's urinal."

126. COMIC STRIP

A well-known reporter, Clark Kent,
Had a simpering, mild-mannered bent.
　　But he grabbed Lois Lane
　　And then made it quite plain
What his cognomen, Superman, meant.

127. ALL THE WAY

There was a young woman of Brest
Who had a magnificent chest.
  When asked if she posed
  With her nipples disclosed,
She said, "Yes—also all of the rest."

128. SEARCH

There was a young woman named Annie
With erogenous zones in each cranny.
  She found this was so
  With the help of her beau,
Who explored her from forehead to fanny.

129. TAKE YOUR TURN

There once was a sweet signorina
Who made one quite glad to have seen 'er.
  To get in, however, you
  Had better endeavor to
Wait in line with a legal subpoena.

130. ASTOUNDING

In Venus, where love's an addiction,
An orgasm's brought on by friction
    Of toes against toes,
    Or nose against nose,
And that's what I call science fiction.

131. FIRST TIME

His first night, Adam said to his dear,
"Darling Eve, you had better stand clear.
    Since touched by your hand
    It's begun to expand
And I don't know how far 'twill uprear."

132. COMFORT

Joe was burrowing one day quite nosily
Down the generous cleavage of Rosalie,
    And, what made it more lewd,
    They were both in the nude
So that they could continue more cozily.

133. TRY IT AGAIN

There was a young fellow of Tulsa,
Who said, "Sex has grown very dull, suh,
  Yet I'm that much a dope,
  If a girl says there's hope
I don't have the heart to repulse 'er."

134. ANATOMICAL CURIOSITY

A certain young woman named Chris
Said, "How odd that young men stand to piss.
  After all, it's less taxing
  And much more relaxing,
Just to sit down, as I do—like this."

135. ESSENTIAL POINT

There was a young fellow named Cliff,
Who said with a yawn, "What's the diff?
  I may not be tall
  And my wealth may be small
But a part of me always stays stiff."

136. JAWOHL

A nostalgic stormtrooper named Schmidt
Used a "Nazi sex practices" kit
    Which had boots and a whip
    With a nice metal tip,
And his bride didn't like it a bit.

137. NOW YOU TELL ME

A certain young lass of Algeria
Was reduced to loud wails of hysteria,
    When her escort one night
    Said, "No, miss, honor bright,
My motives are just not ulterior."

138. PERKING UP THE GATHERING

There was a young fellow named Marty
Who at sex was delightfully hearty.
    With a girl, he'd get in her
    On the floor, during dinner,
And it surely enlivened the party.

139. MACHO

Said a certain curmudgeon named Beecham,
"The ladies? Be certain I'll teach 'em
    To do as I please;
    And if too far to seize,
Never fear. I've a part that will reach 'em."

140. OOH, LA, LA

There was a young lady named Mimi
Who said, "Oh, my dear, you should see me
    In bed with two guys.
    Yet that's not the prize,
It's even more pleasant to be me."

141. IT CAN'T HURT

There was a young woman named Frances
Who decided to better her chances
    By cleverly adding
    Appropriate padding
To enlarge all her protuberances.

142. IT'S MORE USEFUL

An intelligent whore from Albania
Read books and grew steadily brainier.
    Yet it wasn't her science
    That brought her male clients
But her quite uncontrolled nymphomania.

143. WATCH OUT!

It was nice, thought a young man named Max,
To find someone's wife, and relax.
    Yet from such situations
    Can arise complications.
Here's her husband! Good heavens, make tracks!

144. JOHN CIARDI AND I

There is something about satyriasis
That arouses psychiatrists' biases,
    But we're both very pleased
    We're in this way diseased
As the damsel who's waiting to try us is.

Limericks: Too Gross by John Ciardi

1.

There was a young man from Montrose
Who said to a girl, "I propose
    That since time is short
    For affairs of this sort
We begin by removing our clothes."

2.

There was a young lady who wouldn't.
Her mother had told her she shouldn't.
    When dear mama died
    She felt free. So she tried,
But by then she was so old she couldn't.

3.

There was a young lady of Mass
Rather lacking, we all thought, in class.
    She would stroll Boston Common
    And whenever she saw men
She'd whimper, "Please, sir, make a pass."

4.

There was a young man from Belle Isle
Who said to his girl, "If you'll, I'll."
    "I'm willing," said she,
    "But first I must see
How you look as I walk down the aisle."

5.

There once was a smooth-talking Druid
Whose manner of living was luid.
    He'd engage Druid lasses
    In small talk—no passes,
But the first thing they knew they'd been scruid.

6.

A candidate known for his bulsh
Gave a speech so incredibly fulsh
    That I give you my word
    The like's not been heard
Since Harding, or maybe Cal Culsh.

7.

There once was a girl from Red Hook
Who said, "Though I could be mistook,
    One more time ought to do
    To get me and you
Into Guinness's World Record Book."

8.

There was a young lady named Wright
Who simply could not sleep at night
    Because of the ping-
    Ping-ping of her spring
And the glare of her little red light.

9.

To his girl said a Cornish marine,
"You've the knobbiest coastline I've seen.
    'Twould be wonderful sport
    To put into port
—If the rest of the fleet hadn't been."

10.

There was a young lady named Laura
Whom the mere thought of sex filled with haura.
        You may think that *de trop*,
        But I want you to know
That the pope and his crowd were all faura.

11.

A pious old lady of Brewster
Forgave all who'd ever abewster,
        But flew into a rage
        Time could not assuage
When she thought of one cad who'd refewster.

12.

A horrible brat from Belgravia
Drove his parents to thoughts of Our Savia.
        "By Jesus," they swore,
        "We can't stand much more
Of this son of a bitch's behavia!"

13.

A luscious young R.N. from Florida
Found that doctors just couldn't be horrida.
    They pounced on her date
    With a young graduate
And stretched her interne in the corrida.

14.

Cleopatra, when sex was still new to her,
Kept buying up young slaves to tutor her.
    But the Pharaoh (her dad),
    For fear she'd go bad,
Kept rendering them neuterer and neuterer.

15.

There once was a girl from New Haven
Whose pubic hair was not shaven
    But missing because
    She slept without drawers
Within range of a nest-building raven.

16.

There once was a bra Scottish sentry
Who was standing his post in the entry
    When the queen saw his stature
    And, yielding to nature,
She soon made him one of the gentry.

17.

Said Sophocles, putting his X
To the contract for *Oedipus Rex*,
    "I predict it will run
    Until the Year One,
If the shooting script plays up the sex."

18.

Said a salty old skipper of Wales,
"Number One, it's all right to chew nails.
    It impresses the crew.
    It impresses me too.
But stop spitting holes in the sails."

19.

A fallen young lady of fashion
Gave vents to all sorts of base passion.
    Was she scorned? She was not,
    For her ways brought a lot
Of highly respectable cash in.

20.

There was a young fellow named Hodge
Who lured girls to his dear-hunting lodge.
    Once they were there,
    He made them hunt bare.
Serves them right—it's a corny old dodge.

21.

There was a young man from the Nile
Whose amours lacked savoir and style.
    He preferred open country
    And brazen effrontery
To the wiles of conventional guile.

22.

There was an old lady named Clarke
Who didn't look bad in the dark.
    In the first mists of dawn
    She looked haggard and wan.
In the full light of day she looked—stark!

23.

A young ghost from old Bangladesh
Went out with a girl and got fresh.
    Said she, "I don't mind
    High spirits, you'll find,
But I won't have you come in the flesh."

24.

There was a young lady from Hannibal
Who won local fame as a cannibal
    By eating her mother,
    Her father, her brother,
And her two sisters, Gertrude and Annabel.

25.

There was an old maid from Cape Hatteras
Who found one night pinned to her matteras,
    A short basic list
    Of things she had missed
With a lengthy P.S. of et ceteras.

26.

On her high horse, a lady named Hopper
Declared she would let no man topper.
    Till Freddy the Fink,
    Having plied her with drink,
Slipped her cinch—and did she come a cropper!

27.

There was a young lady named Jo
Who always said, "Thank you, but no,"
    Which is poised and polite
    But never does quite
As well as, "Sure, Buster, let's go."

28.

There was a young fellow named Phil
Who was screwing a girl—as boys will.
    She had a girl's knack
    For screwing right back.
The instinct's not easy to kill.

29.

It took me some time to agree
To appear in a film about me
    And my various ex-wives
    Detailing our sex lives,
But I did—and they rated it G.

30.

"My dear unwed mother," said Clancy,
"Met a bounder who tickled her fancy.
    Her fancy thus tickled
    Caused prickles: thus prickled—
Well, you know the rest. Life is chancy."

31.

There was a young madam, a peach,
Who would lure groups of men from the beach.
    When she got them indoors
    She'd phone various whores
And collect a commission from each.

32.

There was a young fellow named Fred
Who took a young lady to bed,
    Then slept the night through,
    Neglecting to do
What her mother had taught her to dread.

33.

A newly found Latin inscription
Refers to a learned Egyptian
    Who at age CCX
    Still indulged in wild sex
After taking a secret prescription.

34.

Said a learned old man of Brabant,
"The instinct, my dear, is extant:
    The extension's extinct.
    Or to be more succinct:
I would if I could, but I can't."

35.

Said a thrice-tested young man named Landis,
"Don't mourn, dear. You know how a gland is.
    If you'll just use your head,
    You'll find *limp* is not *dead:*
It will still serve *mutatis mutandis.*"

36.

An ill-advised salesman named Wade
Made a stop in Kentucky and played
    With a girl in the hay
    Till he heard someone say,
"Step aside, Sis," and "Mistah, yoah daid!"

37.

Our neighborhood whore is no beauty.
But we're not the sort to be snooty.
    We favor a lass
    With a good country ass
And a proper devotion to duty.

38.

There once was a lady named Billie
Who wandered through life willy-nilly
    In aimless affairs
    With chance millionaires
Whose trinkets made marriage look silly.

39.

Said a middle-aged housewife named Pratt,
"Can you damned men think only of *that?*
    Put it back in your pants!"
    "So much for romance,"
Said her husband, "Go shit in your hat!"

40.

Slim, the wrangler, went into cahoots
With a girl to indulge in pursuits
    Unchaste and clandestine
    Which began by divestin'
Themselves of their red union suits.

41.

Here lies an old stinker from Stoneham.
I can't say I'm glad to have known 'im—
    He was filthy, a cheat,
    A rat-fink, a dead beat—
But *de mortuis nil nisi bonum.*

42.

There was an old geezer who tried
All night long, as a matter of pride.
    By dawn's early light
    He whispered, "Goodnight,"
And went into the bathroom and cried.

43·

A pointless old miser named Quince
Spent a lifetime in skinning his flints.
    When the last flint was skun
    He said, "Well, that's done,"
And dropped dead, which he's been ever since.

44·

There's a girl there on Marathon Key
Who gave my pal Flip the V.D.
    Evil ways are a curse.
    Still, it might have been worse:
Had it come heads, it would have been me.

45·

There was a young lady named Meg
Who liked to put boys up a peg.
    Said she, "I don't mind.
    I like to be kind.
And I hate to see young fellows beg."

46.

A clever young fellow named Taft
Caught his death in a Vietnamese draft.
     His last words were, "Shit,
     I've been shot!" Which shows wit.
I wonder why nobody laughed.

47.

There was a young lady so forward,
Especially when she was borward,
     That passing by chance
     I could see at a glance
She was thinking of something untoward.

48.

There's a poor teeny-bopper in Wichita
Whose parents do nothing but bitchita.
     They want her to wait
     For a good proper mate,
But how can she when she's all a-twichita?

49.

An eager young cop from Latrobe
Was assigned by the DA to probe
    Into organized vice.
    Which he did. But the price
Was the worst case of pustules since Job.

50.

There was a young man with a rod
Who thought he'd been chosen by God
    To exercise Hell
    From the girls. He meant well,
But the Thunder said: "*Exorcise*—clod!"

51.

There once was a girl from Haw Creek
Whose virtue left something to seek.
    Our young men all sought it
    And most of them bought it,
Though some only came by to peek.

52.

There was a young fellow named Spiegel
Who had an affair with a seagull
    What's worse—do you see?—
    It wasn't a she
But a he-gull—and *that* is illegal.

53.

There once was a startled young Syrian
Who coming home late, and who peering in
    The window to coo
    To his wife, beheld two
Rather lithe Lebanese disappearyin'.

54.

There was a young lady who knew
She had chosen the wrong thing to do.
    But she did it so well
    She owned a hotel
In Miami before she was through.

55.

A spritely young lady named Wise
One midsummer evening gave rise
    To a chain of events
    Involving six gents
In a general unzipping of flies.

56.

There once was a girl—a humdinger—
Around whom the boys liked to linger
    While babbling of love,
    But got nowhere. "Go shove!"
She would say as she gave them the finger.

57.

At Fred's flat a bouncy young whore
Started bouncing about on the floor.
    "That does it!" said Fred.
    "Now you've busted the bed!"
And dismounted. And showed her the door.

5 8 .

There was an old fellow from Keene
Who dropped dead betwixt and between
  Two bundles of hay
  On each of which lay
What New Hampshiremen call a "sireen."

5 9 ·

That efficient young harlot at Gorms
Made us fill out "New Customer Forms"
  On "Position desired . . . . .
  Equipment required . . . ."
And "Other (State Norms and Ab-
  norms . . . .)."

6 o .

There was a young lady from Putney
Who was given to sexual gluttony.
  Warned a pious old duffer,
  "Your morals will suffer."
"That's what you think," she said. "I ain't gutney."

61.

An antichurch harlot named Rhonda
Keeps tempting our young monks to wander
    From true rectitude
    By walking in nude
And saying, "Behold thy Golconda!"

62.

A dashing young fellow from Alder
Used to spiel such a pure line of folder-
    O-leary-o-lie,
    Our maids would near die.
But time passed and his dash became balder.

63.

Remember the night in Shanghai
When we put down two gallons of rye
    And all eight of the ladies
    At Singapore Sadie's?
—How the days of our youth hurry by!

64.

There was a young lady of parts.
Not one of your lower-class tarts—
    She had worked at St. Johns
    Under ten learned dons
And been certified Mistress of Arts.

65.

A bellhop I met in D.C.
Got all his sex services free.
    He patrolled corridors
    Simply tapping on doors
And replying, "Hell, honey, it's me!"

66.

Said the dean, "I don't care what you think
Of the depths to which others may sink,
    But when I go down
    And you tell the whole town
That I did, then, young man—you're a fink!"

67.

Sir, the chef's in a bit of a stew.
When that waitress at post number 2
    Comes into the kitchen
    He's so busy hitchin'
His pants, that he burns the ragout.

68.

A middle-aged lady named Brewer
Used to ask all the fellows to do her
    A favor of sorts,
    But the number of sports
Who were willing grew fewer and fewer.

69.

There was a masseuse at the club
Who was giving a member a rub.
    Said the member, rubbed red,
    "Please, miss, use your head—
You're rubbing me down to a nub!"

70.

There once was a learned guru
Who found he had nothing to do,
    So he sat on a tack
    And thought into and back
And out and beyond—and clear through.

71.

There once was a stripper who stripped
Until she was barely equipped.
    Said she in chagrin
    As she fingered her skin,
"Good heaven's—this part of it's ripped!"

72.

There was an ex-Wave with a suite
Overlooking the Bay. When the fleet
    Steamed in from maneuvers
    She blinked with her louvers,
"Standing by to be boarded. Repeat:
Standing by to be boarded. Repeat:
Standing by to be boarded. Repeat . . ."

73·

Said her grace, "I impose one condition
Before I assume the position.
    It's my view that nudity
    Cannot excuse crudity.
No fucking. Just tasteful coition."

74·

There was a young lady named Stein
With rondures so nearly divine
    And so few inhibitions
    To set harsh conditions,
That she spent half her life on her spine.

75·

P.S.   The rest of her time, let me add,
        Was not spent in cleaning her pad,
            But prone, or asprawl,
            Or astraddle, but all—
        Nearly all of it—scantily clad.

74

76.

Which saved her a deal of expense.
Thus, by practicing good common sense,
      She made both ends meet
      Though the rent of her suite,
And her lingerie bills, were immense.

77.

There was an old lecherous earl
Who took in a poor homeless girl
      And induced her to sin
      With promises, gin,
And such cant as "Let's give it a whirl!"

78.

There was a young lady named Rose
Who liked to slip out of her clothes
      When receiving a gent,
      Which helped pay the rent
And kept her amused, I suppose.

79.

There was a young lady named Rose
Who liked to slip out of her clothes
    When men came to call.
    "You are welcome to all,"
She would say, striking pose after pose.

80.

Vicar Smedley, our pie-in-the-sky man
Called on Clara and ruptured her hymen
    On the eve of her marriage
    To Tredlowe T. Claridge—
Which I'd say is rather shrewd timin'.

81.

A drunken old tar from Saint Clements,
To ward off the scurvy, sucked lemons.
    "With my health unimpaired,
    I have time," he declared,
"To die of delirium tremens."

8 2 .

A personnel person from Cobb
Was giving a young man the job.
  Said she, "I can tell
  You will do very well.
You're a young man who uses his knob."

8 3 .

There was a young lady from Lester
Who allowed all the boys to molest her.
  She was gentle and kind,
  But those traits, you may find,
Spread diseases that burn, itch, and fester.

8 4 .

As Dame Eleanor came through the door,
Her chambermaid leaped from the floor,
  Interrupting coition.
  "What a curious position!"
Said the dame, "May I see it once more?"

8 5.

A young mountain climber named Frazier
Fell into a crack in a glacier.
    "This is really appalling!"
    He shouted while falling,
Then lapsed into total aphasia.

8 6.

There was a young lady from Brest
Whom the curé once put to the test
    By letting her see
    How bleak sin could be,
But she wasn't the least bit impressed.

8 7.

"Yes, of course," said a girl from Latrop,
"But it's hard to know quite where to stop.
    A boy lifts your slip.
    Then you hear him unzip.
Then what do you do?—call a cop?"

88.

There was a young fellow so poor
He lived in a half-furnished sewer.
    He never complained
    Though at times—when it rained—
He did find life hard to endure.

89.

At the Pan-Hell Olympics last week
The second prize went to a Deke.
    Amid mounting applause
    From the third-place Psi Taus
He laid eighteen girls cheek to cheek.

90.

There's a lady in suite 7-C
Who allowed two young men to make free
    Till she heard someone say,
    "That's all for today."
And discovered she'd been on TV.

91.

There was a young lady whose taste
Ran to chain mail and locks 'round the waist.
>   She was charming, I'd say,
>   In a general way,
But rather obsessively chaste.

92.

An insomniac young fellow named Hatches
Took a room in a whorehouse in Natchez.
>   He still tossed and turned
>   Half the night, but he learned
How to manage by sleeping in snatches.

93.

A widow of some fashion kept
A young lout in her bed while she slept.
>   She would smile when she woke
>   To finger his spoke,
And think, "This lacks couth, but it's ept."

94.

Said Socrates, keeping his poise,
"Tell Xanthippe I've done with her noise.
    If she asks what you mean,
    Just say, when last seen
I was drinking with some of the boys."

95.

On the talk show last night, Dr. Ellis,
The sex shrink, took two hours to tell us
    It's all right to enjoy
    A rosy-cheeked boy
So long as your sheep don't get jealous.

96.

There was a stout lad of the fleet
In Cherbourg, in the chips, and in heat.
    He bought out La Maison
    De Madame de Bonbon,
And kept calling for girls toot-de-sweet.

97.

There was a male chauvinist pig
Who bought a stuffed bra and a wig
    And started rehearsin'
    To be a chairperson
In case Bella Abzug won big.

98.

One dark night a lady from Snelling
Awoke with a curious swelling
    In the palm of her hand.
    It was—yes—a male gland.
But whose, she had no way of telling.

99.

There once was a diddlesome lass
Whose dandles drew young men *en masse*.
    What with diddling and dandling
    She endured much manhandling—
Rather more than most girls of her class.

1 0 0 .

There once was a girl who used paint
On her navel. Her boyfriend said, "Ain't
    That going too far?"
    "No more than you are,"
She said. "Do I hear a complaint?"

1 0 1 .

There was a young man at Twin Lakes
With a terrible case of the shakes.
    He writhed on the lawn
    From midnight to dawn
Like Laocoön, but with more snakes.

1 0 2 .

A young baseball groupie named Ritter
Will soon need a good babysitter.
    She couldn't say no
    To the sluggers, and so
She got hit, but she can't say what hitter.

103.

Said an airy young lady from Metz
Who kept ordering more crêpes suzettes,
    "Of course I don't eat them
    But nothing can beat them
For a posh way to light cigarettes."

104.

Have you heard about Mrs. Cotell?
She checked into the Eden Motel
    For a blissful weekend
    With the friend of a friend,
But when she got home she caught Hell.

105.

There was a young wife from Peoria
Who checked into the Waldorf-Astoria
    Where she stayed for a week
    With two Swedes and a Greek
In a state of near-total euphoria.

106.

Said Miguel to the gringo, "Señor,
Eef I open these here closet door,
    An' dee lady eenside
    Ees my leetle lost bride,
Than I theenk I mus' shoot you some more."

107.

Said a girl who was forced to go dutch
On a love nest, "I don't mind too much.
    Though I pay half the lease,
    I collect half—apiece—
From Smitty, Gil, Stu, Tim, and Hutch."

108.

Said Calpurnia, "Though I must render
Unto Caesar the brunt of my gender,
    A few side effects
    Are permitted my sex
When we're feeling illegally tender."

109.

There was a young fellow from Bingham
Whose girl had to run off and bring 'im
 A new set of tweeds
 While he hid in the weeds
Where he'd lost his while jigging her thingum.

110.

A toast to the lady vice cop
With the most busts for trying to stop
 The tide of ill-doing
 In pay-for-play screwing—
Undercover, she came out on top!

111.

"Yes, mother, it's starting to show,"
Said Nell, "But no use blaming Joe.
 And I doubt it was Fred,
 Or the vicar, or Ned.
The fact is, I simply don't know."

112.

"Is it too much to ask," said Lord Rayne
To a baggage with whom he had lain,
    "That you wait below stairs
    And tend your affairs,
In case I require you again?"

113.

What a temperate man Dr. Wise is.
When three coeds in silly disguises
    Leaped on him in bed,
    He did not scold. He said,
"Very well, then. But no more surprises!"

114.

There was a young fellow named Shear
Who stuck a ballpoint in his ear.
    When he punctured the drum
    He said, "That hurts some,
But the rest of the way through is clear."

115.

Said a wicked old madam named Belle
Whom the preacher was threatening with Hell,
    "I have no regrets,
      No doubts—and no debts.
If I haven't done good, I've done well."

116.

There once was an Arab so poor
He was forced by the neighborhood whore
    To trade his left nut
      For a night with the slut,
Who dried it to hang on her door.

117.

The Tri-Delts are under a cloud.
When their housemother, Mrs. Van Dowd,
    Either quit or retired,
      They seem to have hired
A stripteaser—which isn't allowed.

118.

There was a young pilot from Bangor
Who locked eighteen girls in his hangar
    Where he treated them wrong
    And kept them so long
The countryside rose up in anger.

119.

A conservative lady named Tabor
Had a date with her radical neighbor.
    They argued all night
    On the left and the right.
In the end, though, he brought her to labor.

120.

There once was a girl from Bermuda
Who undressed till she couldn't be nuda.
    When one young man inquired
    Why she wasn't attired,
She said, "Can't you be a bit cruda?"

121.

A young public steno from Surrey
Did her work well with never a worry.
    Though her clients were myriad
    She did not miss a period,
For she never did things in a hurry.

122.

A shepherd who came from Bangkok
Used to dabble in watered-down stock.
    His peculiar perversion
    Was total immersion
Till he drowned all the sheep in his flock.

123.

There was a young lady named Candy
Who made do, when no boys were handy,
    With a girlfriend or two—
    Sometimes Betty Lou,
But more often Belinda and Mandy.

124.

> Said a hesitant youth from Siberia,
> "If it please you to, uh, try, my dearie, uh,
>   This, uh, thingumbob
>   Is what, uh, does the job
> When it's thrust into, uh, your interia."

125.

> An efficient young lady of Rome
> Began to do piecework at home.
>   Eight hours a day,
>   Fifteen minutes a lay,
> Neatly timed by the chimes from the Dome.

126.

> A young handyman from Biloxi
> Tried coating his tool with epoxy.
>   In practice he found—
>   Though his theory was sound—
> It was rather like screwing by proxy.

1 2 7 .

"No! No!" said a man so penurious
He'd convinced himself sex was injurious,
     "At a pretty a penny
     I wouldn't have any.
At tuppence, I'm not even curious."

1 2 8 .

There was a magician named Carr
Who used to be billed as a star.
     His future looked sweet
     Till he walked down the street
And—*presto!*—turned into a bar.

1 2 9 .

A wandering minstrel named Gay
Got a girl in the family way.
     Her brother and dad
     Rode after the cad.
And that was the minstrel's last lay.

130.

There was a young devil named Stu
Who ruined a maiden or two.
　　That is, if good screwin'
　　Can cause a girl's ruin.
Even so—give the devil his due.

131.

The late poet Wystan Hugh Aud'n
Left us poems never maudl'n but mod'n.
　　The first things he wrote
　　Struck a socialist note,
But increasingly then he let God'n.

132.

I know an old harlot named Triskett
So broad in the rump and the brisket
　　That since she began
　　To solicit, no man
Has said "Let's go!" but only "I'll risk it!"

133.

There was a young fellow from Kent
Who drank till he grew redolent.
    He wasn't so rank
    You could quite say he stank,
But downwind he gave off quite a scent.

134.

I don't give a damn, by and large,
About sex. There's too much persiflage
    In dating and bedding
    And, worst of all, wedding.
It just doesn't give me a charge.

135.

There was a young man of Des Moines
Who made rather too much of his groin.
    "Make a bid," he would shout
    As he flashed it about.
"OK, Ladies—Going . . . going . . . goin'!"

136.

I doubt that much more will be heard
Of Agatha Margaret MacBird.
    She was last seen in Berks
    With two businesslike Turks
Who were peddling her off to a third.

137.

There was a young fellow named Pfister
Who noticed an odd sort of blister
    Where no blister should be.
    What was worse—do you see?—
He had got it at home from his sister.

138.

I was told by a mathematician
That the odds against having coition
    With Betty Jo Donne
    Are a hundred to one.
So they are—till you ask her permission.

139.

A pious young maiden named Dexter
Prayed so long that it damn near desexed 'er.
    Yet, though she prayed hard,
    Her mind, when off guard,
Churned up visions that vexed and perplexed 'er.

140.

There once was an upcoming lad.
Full of juice, but a bit of a cad.
    Once he got off his rocks
    He would put on his socks
And sneer, "Well, I guess you've been had!"

141.

A devout but ambiguous maid
Liked to play with the boys. Having played
    She feared (some) for her soul
    But believed on the whole
She was not lost but only mislaid.

142.

I feel sorry for young Dr. Dow.
Our ladies won't go to him now.
  When examining the parts
  Of Mrs. Ray Hartz
He should have said "Hmmm" and not "Wow!"

143.

I said to the neighborhood whore,
"How's my credit?" She showed me the door.
  It gets hard for a bloke
  When he's friendless and broke,
But I guess that's the fate of the poor.

144.

At a serious bar in Bel Air
A lady walked in and stood bare.
  She kept leering and winking.
  But drinking is drinking,
And not one man noticed her there.

145.

There was a young lady from Rye
Who was roundly misused by a guy.
    She did not feel abused
    At being so used.
She was happy to give it a try.

146.

There was a young lady named Burr
Who, when dating, wore nothing but fur.
    When she slipped off her coat
    She would say—and I quote—
"I hope I am causing a stir."

147.*

Said a voice from the back of the car,
"Young man, I don't know who you are.
    But allow me to state,
    Though it may come too late,
I had not meant to go quite this far."

* PUBLISHER'S NOTE:
  Mr. Ciardi appears to have cheated and gone over his gross limit.
  In his defense let it be noted that the three extras are little more
  than addenda, or explanations, or variations, or warts on three
  others of his collection.

Foreword III
by Isaac Asimov

How John Ciardi Grew Engrossed

The question I am most frequently asked is: "Asimov, how do you manage to make up your deliciously crafted limericks?"

It's difficult to find an answer that doesn't sound immodest, since "Sheer genius!" happens to be the truth.

It's terrible when you have to choose between the virtues of honesty and of modesty. Generally I choose honesty, which is one way (among many) in which I am different from John Ciardi. Not that I mean to impugn John's character, of course.

I am sure he would choose honesty, too, if he knew what it was.

The last time someone asked him how *he* managed to compose limericks, John said, "What are limericks?"

But then, John is still young (seventy-nine, I think, judging from his appearance) and he may yet learn some of the rudiments of verse, though I understand 3-to-1 odds that he won't learn are being offered and finding no takers.

Another question I am frequently asked is: "How is it you are willing to appear in the same book with John Ciardi?" And to that the only possible answer is "Sheer stupidity!"

Actually, it was not my intention to take part in this *mésalliance*, and I had better tell you the whole story.

I had composed, in leisurely style, and with involuted poetic thought, three hundred limericks and had published them in three books (one hundred limericks apiece, for those of you who are mathematically inclined and are trying to divide three hundred by three—something that consistently gives John trouble).

The first was published under the title of *Lecherous Limericks* by Walker and Company. They were not lecherous, of course, but rather delightful; yet Walker turned down the suggestion of *Delightful Limericks* because he said he wanted the alliteration. (That means two L's, John.)

Whereupon I suggested *Lovely Limericks*, *Languorous Limericks*, and *Lilting Limericks* as more truly descriptive and as alliterative as well, but the publisher, a ribald sort, countered with *Lascivious Limericks* and we compromised on *Lecherous*.

When the second book appeared, there was considerable head scratching over a title that would capitalize on the enormous cleverness of the first. No less than seventy-eight possible titles were studied and rejected, including, *The Bride of Lecherous Limericks, Lecherous Limericks Fights Back*, and *Lecherous Limericks in the Black Lagoon*.

At the end of a nineteen-hour marathon session on the subject, we had about settled on *Lecherous Limericks Meets Dracula and the Wolf Man and Abbott and Costello*, when a delivery boy who had just delivered sandwiches said, "Why not call it *More Lecherous Limericks?*"

We threw him out, of course, for compound fracture of the imagination and naturally refused to pay for the sandwiches.

But we decided to use his title, and *More Lecherous Limericks* is what it was. When the third book came out, a mood of exhaustion had enveloped us, and when the publisher said sarcastically, "I suppose you want to call this one *Still More Lecherous Limericks?*" I was astonished at the brilliance of the notion and accepted it at once.

The three books, you can well imagine, set the publishing world ablaze. Far and wide, from sea to shining sea, bookstore clerks all over were saying, with one voice, "Sorry, sir, I never heard of them."

I sat back with satisfaction to enjoy my growing fame as a

lyric poet, taking pleasure at my having joined the ranks of the Shakespeares and the Shelleys. (They're poets, John. Dead ones.)

And that's where John Ciardi comes in.

I had met John Ciardi on occasions in the past. That is, I hadn't exactly met him in the sense that it was a voluntary coming together. Generally, I turned rapidly into a doorway as soon as I saw him, but the trouble is that I am not sufficiently visual. I generally ignore the world around me, being deeply engaged in weaving my creative fancies within the labyrinths of my brain. It followed that by the time the large and impressively rotund figure of J. C. had impressed itself on my mind, he was virtually upon me and it was too late to dodge.

Moving into a doorway was worse than useless, for he merely followed me and there isn't room in the same doorway for John and me . . . or for John and anybody . . . or for John.

Let me explain, by the way, that John, at a loss for any other claim to respectability, had decided to be a poet—or at least to describe himself as such to any policeman who approached him for the obvious purpose of arresting him for aggravated vagrancy in the third degree.

Out of weary politeness, everyone has accepted him at this self-evaluation so that he is regularly described as "Mr. John Ciardi, the self-proclaimed poet-or-something."

You can well imagine that John was irritated in the extreme at my cometlike blaze across the firmament of rhyme and decided to do something about it. He sent me a letter which read:

> Since you've shown you can do it, old pal,
> Then I, also, most certainly shall
> Get exceedingly poetical.

This astonished me, for John's prosody is not usually that skillful.

I found out later that he spent considerable time secluded with my books of limericks, counting syllables and sounding out the rhymes till he thought he could manage a passable imitation.

He then proceeded to write 144 limericks in a gross manner only to find that he couldn't get them published unless the name of an established poet accompanied his.

It was at that point that he got one of the few good ideas he has ever had—perhaps even the only one. He challenged me to do 144 also and join him in a coauthored book.

Caught by surprise, but—by the oddest chance—having a free afternoon, I accepted, and the result was *Limericks: Too Gross*, published by the esteemed gentlemen of W. W. Norton.

John was convinced, I am sure, that the book would prove that he was a more delicately skillful poet than I was, so naturally, it turned out to be a great disappointment for him, poor fellow.

He sent me a note which read . . .

> Very well, my old friend, let us see,
> (If you have one more afternoon free)
> Who can win—the best two out of three

in typical Ciardian verse.

The result is the present volume. I expect a snarled invitation to make it the best three out of five any day now.

—Isaac Asimov

Foreword IV
by John Ciardi

Isaac Asimov: An Appreciation

My respect for Isaac Asimov is a long-standing article of faith: I have been standing for half my life waiting for some reason to arrive in support of my admiration, but it remains, like any article of faith, beyond reason. And well that it is, for I cannot imagine any reason within range of reason to support my quaint regard for him.

Like the earth, the sea, the wind—especially like the wind—the Asimovian presence is an assertion of the primal environment, and the more so as the environment deteriorates. There are times, in fact, when I feel that he is more presence than there is environment for. It will not do to enter his presence until one has placated the first gods. I am empowered by Nil and by Void, by Zilch and by Butkis, and by Framis and Dither, mother and father of Cacophony, to declare that Isaac is the only natural phenomenon capable of rushing in forever to fill his own ever-expanding vacuum.

He has been a horizon line to my life, a constant and necessary point of reference as impressively empty as the far rim of an Oklahoma panorama. Oklahoma once picked up its horizon and blew it away in dust storms. Isaac blows himself away forever. Yet my faith remains that when the storm passes the choking blather will subside and the horizon of some overblown future will once more come into view at the far reaches of the cracked fields.

For there is no evil in the fellow; a talent for inducing nausea, perhaps, but no evil. When, at dank intervals of the soul, I am moved by the Imp of the Perverse to crave pure revulsion, I seek out Isaac's company and he never fails me, for I know that once I have survived the moonscape (dark side) of his wit, I am proof against every desolation of the spirit.

It is not that Isaac's prose is lacking. Nothing in the creation is less lacking. His is a primal blizzard. The utter, blasting overmuchness of it makes nuance impossible and taste irrelevant. Granted such ample qualities in him, what can it matter that he has a tin ear and a sledgehammer touch?

Yet now the fellow, having ridden my coattails to literary splendor by association, has outblown his own bray. He has gone so far as to put words into my mouth. I will not attempt to put any of my words into his: he would not be able to pronounce them. Words, I would have him know, are precious crystals. To put any words of mine into his mouth would be like throwing fine Venetian glass into a wind tunnel, reducing all that might once have trembled in purest tones to crash and splatter.

The art of the limerick (as the truly formal half of this book will make clear) is based on what I will call an ear for chamber music. It is keyed to delicate harmonies and counterpoints, to nuance, and to a seemingly effortless formality and unity.

Isaac has, at best, a fife-and-drum ear. He has learned to boom and to whistle and to strut to the beat, as any robot can. Albert Einstein (a mathematician said by some to rival Isaac Asimov) once remarked that if men were meant only to march they would need no brain, for a merely reflexive spinal cord would suffice for the work. Isaac, in his grasp of such measures, has understood Einstein and has economized accordingly.

These distinctions have been obscured by the sandblast of Asimov's prose. Poetry, however—and even verse—comes contained within a silence and echoes off into the silence that follows. Nothing is more lacking than an Asimovian silence. It is not that the language trembles at his assault upon it, but it does snicker.

Isaac, nevertheless, has a shrewd head up his sleeve, and his performance can be impressive until one stops to think about it. But as Samuel Johnson once remarked of a poodle that danced on his hind legs (I approximate from memory), "To say it is not well done would be a commonplace. The wonder is that it should be attempted."

There remains a point of conscience. I would not willingly defraud any reader. What shall I say to the reader who, having paid for a whole book, finds he has bought only a half book? One might of course razor out Asimov's pages, as neatly as possible, and perhaps recover some of the purchase price by peddling them at a garage sale for illiterates. To razor out Isaac's worthless pages, however, would likely damage the binding that preserves my gemlike offerings. I suggest that the tasteful reader merely skip Isaac's awful oddities and read my perfected forms twice, thus receiving full value, and more —though once the reader comes under the spell of my limericks I find it inconceivable that he could stop at a mere two readings. Yet let me also suggest that the reader's appreciation of my mastery can only be heightened by an occasional glance at the profusions of the robotically admirable Mr.—uh—oh, yes . . . Asimov.

> What Asimov lacks of pure style
> He makes up for—well, once in a while—
> By the way he can bluster
> From the depths of lackluster
> To the (almost) transcendently vile.

John Ciardi
Key West, Florida

A New Gross of Limericks
by Isaac Asimov

1. DON'T STOP NOW

When a certain young lass was still younger,
She requested a fellow to tongue 'er.
> He was two inches deep
> And he then fell asleep;
An event that completely unstrung 'er.

2. HOW IMPOLITE

There was a rude man with a beard
Whose behavior was terribly weird.
> Though he'd screw a long list
> Of girls in the mist
He'd be gone by the time it had cleared.

3. ALL IN THE TECHNIQUE

Said a sweet little damsel, "I blush
At requesting you, sir, not to rush.
> Before pounding the meat
> In a blazing white heat
Why not finger the soft underbrush.

4.   DO YOUR BIT

"My dear," shouted frustrated Wallace,
"Why persist in behavior that's callous?
    Don't just sit there and stare,
    That is mean and unfair
Come and help me unlimpen my phallus!"

5.   SYMMETRY

To moralists, sex is a sin,
Yet Nature suggests we begin.
    She arranged it, no doubt,
    That a fellow juts out
In the place where a damsel juts in.

6.   THAT'S ALL?

There was a young fellow (a cheater)
Who promised a girl he would treat 'er
    To something quite fine,
    Even grand and divine,
And then all he brought forth was his peter.

7 .   WHO WOULDN'T?

There was an old fellow named Ed
Who had a bad cold in the head.
    "When all's said and done,"
      He said, "It's no fun.
I'd prefer a young woman instead."

8 .   ENVIRONMENTAL EFFECT

When alone, a young woman named Julia
Had qualities rather peculiar.
    And when men were about
    (Short, tall, lean, or stout)
Her conduct was even unrulier.

9 .   WELL, HE'S NEAT

Said a certain prim fellow named Hess,
"Though it causes a bit of distress,
    I avoid the last spasm
    Of completed orgasm.
I simply can't stand all that mess."

10. SHE'S GOT GUTS

A shy little thing from Canberra
Decided that sex was an erra.
 It scared her to bits,
 It drove her to fits,
But she did it—in fear and in terra.

11. CONCENTRATION

An ardent young fellow named Dutton
Was simply a sexual glutton.
 He would always make hay
 Nine or ten times a day,
And aside from all that, he did nuttin'.

12. IT ANNOYS THE KING

A courtier, in dazzling array,
Screwed the Queen (Anne Boleyn) one fine day.
 He got little credit.
 He was promptly beheaded,
For the clear crime of *lays majesté*.

13. CRASH!

On a bridge that went 'cross a ravine
Archibald had been screwing Kathleen.
    The force of his lunge
    Caused the whole thing to plunge.
The worst fucking disaster I've seen.

14. WHY WASTE TIME?

A water boy named Gunga Din
Always wore not much more than his skin.
    Such a costume lacked class,
    But on meeting a lass
He was able, at once, to plunge in.

15. PARTY TIME

"Here we are," said Attila the Hun,
"Won't you join us in all of the fun?
    We'll slaughter and pillage
    Every last helpless village.
Come quickly, the action's begun."

16. CITIES OF THE PLAIN

A Biblical worthy named Lot
Lived out where the action was hot.
    Those guys out in Sodom?
    Other guys had all rode 'em,
Till God noticed and said, "Thou shalt not."

17. WASTED EFFORT

A deplorable fellow named Sloane
Once called twenty girls on the phone.
    He asked each if they'd screw.
    Each replied, "Nuts to you."
So the poor guy sits home all alone."

18. THAT FINAL TOUCH

Said a cheerful young woman of Graz,
Who made love on the flimsiest cots.
    "With the final hup-hup
    The whole thing just folds up,
And it's fun to end up tied in knots."

19. PREVENTIVE MEDICINE

Said another young woman of Graz
"You ask how much screwing? Why, lots!
    About ten to fourteen
    With perversions between.
Any less and I break out in spots."

20. JUST LINE UP

There once was a wicked old squire
Who burned with libidinous fire.
    After screwing a nun
    And the minister's son,
He took on all the girls in the choir.

21. GOOD FOR NOTHING

Said a fading old lecher named Cardigan,
"I'm afraid that I'll never get hard again.
    What's more, the girls know
    I've this trouble, and so
At the local bordellos, I'm barred again."

2 2 . WRONG!

It was just like old Lester one day
When he joined a young woman in play
        To fail in recalling
        How to go about balling,
So he did the whole thing the wrong way.

2 3 . CONTINOUS CREATION

An astronomess happily sang,
"I've been screwed by the telescope gang,
        They all had a bit o' me,
        For I'm the epitome
Of the grandly impressive Big Bang."

2 4 . IT CAN'T BE SO!

Our delicate verses, limerickal,
So frequently seem anticlerical.
        Each saintly old minister
        Is made to seem sinister
And is filled with a lust quite hysterical.

25. WRONG TIME

There was an old fellow named Morey
And this is his sorrowful story.
    He screwed each of a myriad
    Damsels during her period;
And, gosh, did the bedclothes get gory.

26. SPLASH!!!

Love and sex among mammals aquatic
Is seldom, if ever, quite static.
    When the giant sperm whale
    Impales his female
The results are both loud and dramatic.

27. TO EACH HIS OWN

A New Jerseyite born in Paramus
Offered all of us one of life's dramas.
    He went to the zoo
    And before a long queue
Of men, he screwed one of the llamas.

28. NOBODY'S PERFECT

"The trouble with me," poor old Jack said,
"Is that though my mustache has been wax-ed,
    And I've gook in my hair,
    And I'm devil-may-care,
The fact is that my penis is flaccid."

29. THEY'RE SUPPOSED TO

There was once an unbalanced he-rabbit
Who had the deplorable habit
    Of viewing the cunny
    Of each nice female bunny,
Then using his pee-pee to jab it.

30. ORGY TIME

There was a young fellow named Pete
Who hastened to Plato's Retreat;
    But the girl he would ride
    Had each hole occupied
So he rubbed his poor prick on her feet.

31. LOVELY!

There once was a gorgeous young girl
Who kept the men's heads in a whirl.
  Her long pubic hair
  Was resilient and fair
And her nipples were mother-of-pearl.

32. PANT, PANT

There was a tall, gorgeous Valkyrie
Who found her admirers grew leery.
  When they climb to the spot
  Where the action is hot,
They cannot dip in; they're too weary.

33. WHY WATCH THE SCREEN?

An exhibiting fellow from Truro,
Underpaid in a government bureau,
  Earned additional dough
  With a public sex show
At the movie house, back in the U-row.

3 4 . VA - VA - VA -VOOM

An intelligent lass named Jo Anne
Never lacked an admiring young man
    For her giant IQ
    (Giant other things, too)
Was designed on a generous plan.

3 5 . NO FUN IN THAT

There once was a handsome young pianist
Whose views about girls were the cle-anest.
    He placed one and all
    On a high pedestal,
And the women all thought him the me-anest.

3 6 . STANDING OVATION

There was a young woman named Dawes
Whose costume was made all of gauze.
    When they turned on the light
    Behind her one night,
All the fellows broke into applause.

37. SERVED HIM RIGHT

A young fellow who drove a Mercedes
Was a terrible lech with the ladies.
 What with all his misleading
 He had raptures exceeding,
But he died—and went straight down to Hades.

38. IT'S ALL IN THE MIND

There was a young man so obscene,
He would chuckle at words like "between."
 "Between legs," "between lips,"
 "Between breasts," "between hips."
There wasn't a use he found clean.

39. BOOKKEEPING

A methodical fellow named Wade
Could recall every girl that he'd laid.
 He recorded each poke,
 Every thrust, every stroke,
And precisely how much he'd been paid.

40. WHAT'S MONEY?

A generous damsel named Marge,
When she spied one delightfully large,
    Would kick up her heels
    And, spurning all deals,
Take care of the thing without charge.

41. NONCHALANCE

Once a pretty young woman named Marjorie,
Having dinner within a potagerie,
    Had soup-stained her dress
    And, without much distress,
Took it off, and ate on in her lingerie.

42. PRACTICE

There once was an eager young nurse
Who felt that she had to rehearse
    Every sexual joy,
    Every hot little ploy,
To succeed in becoming perverse.

43. MIND YOUR OWN BUSINESS

There was a young woman named Linda
Who did it in front of the winda.
    The guys passing by
    Would give her the eye
But she didn't allow it to hinda.

44. NOT FAIR

Young Sadie keeps books at bordellos
And she's sore as can be at the fellows.
    All the others turn tricks,
    Get their fill of men's pricks,
But Sadie just gets polite hellos.

45. SUPER-MIDAS

A rollicking fellow named Rex
Was under a fortunate hex.
    It seems he had such
    An unusual touch
It turned everything into sex.

46. IT'S POSSIBLE

A well-brought-up woman named Kay
Would frown, and then haughtily say,
    "If we're speaking of sin
    I will never begin
And yet—well, perhaps—I just may."

47. TRÈS BIEN

There was an old man of Marseilles
Who said to a demoiselle, "Heilles,
    I'll pay you beaucoup
    Give you jewelry, toup,
If only you'll do it my weilles."

48. THERE'S A LINE

With a smile said the lass of Marseilles,
"I admit it's my business to pleille,
    But voilà tout les hommes
    All waiting to commes,
So I cannot oblige you todeilles."

49. FEARLESS

Central Park was the site of the pass.
"Very well! Here and now!" said the lass.
    Did the fellow then flee
    Pusillanimously?
No! He screwed her right there on the grass.

50. THE TABLE ROUND

There was once a great knight named Sir Lancelot
Who placed Queen Guinevere in a trance a lot.
    But what bothered the King
    Was: he managed the thing
By serenely removing his pants a lot.

51. DEPENDS ON THE CONDITIONS

There's a certain young woman named Barb
Who at casual sex is a darb,
    But put her to the test
    And you'll find she's her best
When completely divested of garb.

5 2 . WHOLESALE

There once was a roguish young lass
Who excelled in biology class.
 She thought it was fun
 To curl up with one,
But terrific to do it *en masse*.

5 3 . UNDER COVER

A young lass from the far-off Laurentians
Once made love in a bed of fringed gentians,
 Where the deeds that she did
 Were so much better hid.
They're perversions, you see, no one mentions.

5 4 . FERTILITY RITE

A fine lassie from Auld Edinboro
Was once screwed in a freshly turned furrow.
 To encourage fertility
 With all her ability,
She tried hard as she could to be thorough.

5 5 . P U R I T Y

A conception that should be immaculate
Will in no way involve an ejaculate.
    But where is the fun
    If that is so done?
For myself, I just don't care to tackle it.

5 6 . W I S E O L D D O C

A kindly old doctor named Grover
Once said, "I am clearly in clover.
    Not being a fool
    I use my own tool
Whenever I'm probing for ova."

5 7 . V A R I E T Y

There was a young woman named Cora Lee
Who said, "I will do it immorally
    On top and on bottom,
    Any way that I've got 'em,
Vaginally, anally, orally."

58. ABILITY

In considering active coition
Good girls scorn to impose a condition.
    They let it be known
    They have but to be shown
To adopt any wanted position.

59. OBLIGING

To her boyfriend said pretty Jeanette,
"There are no conditions, my pet.
    You may use any surface,
    Any bump, any orifice,
Whatsoever you want, I am set."

60. TASTY

There was a young woman named Jenny (yum, yum),
Whose charms were delightful and many (yum, yum),
    The sight of her boobs
    And the taste of her pubes
Seemed to herald the coming millennium (yum).

6 1 .   IT'S THE SAME IN RUSSIA

There was a young lass of Odessa
Who said to her father confessor,
    "When the fellows surround me
    Pursue me and hound me,
Do you think I give in to them? Yes, sir."

6 2 .   DANCING CHEEK TO CHEEK

Ginger Rogers and suave Fred Astaire
Made one hell of a fine dancing pair.
    She had such sex appeal
    But did he cop a feel?
But of course not! The Thirties were square!

6 3 .   EXPERIENCE

My boy, don't get married too soon
To do it's the act of a loon.
    It's all right to play
    In the great month of May,
But a wedding takes place in Jejune.

6 4 . W H E W !

To wed four wives at once is Islamic
And yet, on the whole, not so comic.
    To satisfy four
    Is a bone-breaking chore
Unless your sex drive is atomic.

6 5 . V E R S A T I L E

There was a young fellow whose staff
Was, in inches, some twelve and a half.
    It was used as a cue,
    As a baseball bat, too,
(Which always produced a good laugh).

6 6 . T O E A C H H I S O W N

There was a young man of La Jolla*
Who kept screwing his wife in the folla.
    Those who passed by would mumble
    Or stub toes and stumble
But the folla was where he'd enjolla.

* pronounced "la hoyuh"

67. THAT TIME OF THE MONTH

Said a woman from old San José
To her lover, embarrassed, "Oh, say,
    This vagina of mine
    You say is like wine—
But today, I'm afraid, it's rosé.

68. DEMOCRACY

Many think it is quite egotistic
To have sex that is just onanistic.
    Most people would choose
    To do it in twos,
Since our system should stay pluralistic.

69. WHAT DO YOU EXPECT?

A Back Bay attorney named Kyle
Kept a very elaborate file
    On the sexual habits
    Of Lowells and Cabots
And found them surprisingly vile.

132

70. CURRENT PERMISSIVENESS

Through the length and the breadth of this nation
All's now proper on every occasion.
    If a woman feels able,
    Then under the table
Is a suitable place for fellation.

71. NATURAL CONSEQUENCE

A publisher, once (name of Knopf),
Alas, never knew when to stopf.
    He lay down on the hipf
    Of a charming young pipf,
And now he's a charming old popf.

72. BUSY LITTLE FELLOW

An ardent young lecher named Joel
Found himself a most interesting goal:
    To screw all the gals
    Of each of his pals
From the day before New Year to Noel.

73. OMITTED

"Good God, what a terrible flap'll
Be caused by that one bite of apple."
    Said the Lord—but that frolic
    Was sex (quite symbolic)
—That's not shown in the old Sistine Chapel.

74. OVERENTHUSIASTIC

To his bride said young Galahad, "Kiddo,
Let's screw in each room, beach, and meadow,
    Every day, every night,
    In the dark, in the light."
And they tried it, and now she's a widow.

75. WON'T FIT

Said a certain young well-endowed Finn,
"I can never do more than begin.
    Though I try very hard,
    My attempt is ill-starred,
I can *not* shove it all the way in."

76. AMATEUR TALENT

Mused a certain young woman named Joan,
"I suppose that I'm never alone,
    Since I'm such a good lay
    And I never ask pay
And that somehow the fact's become known."

77. NO, NO, NOT THAT!

There was an ingenuous Lapp
Who was, it appeared, quite a sapp.
    When a young woman said,
    "Please come to my bed."
He thanked her and took a long napp.

78. UPHOLDING MY HONOR

Some young women once had the audacity
To impugn my erotic capacity.
    I stilled all their doubts
    With erotical bouts
And thus proved my colossal first-classity.

79. THOSE MEDITERRANEANS

Getting girls for the fellows from Sicily
Involves acts that are winky and whistly.
    But all over Italy
    Fathers then react fitally,
And go after them knify and missily.

80. THAT'S A LONG DISTANCE

A girl from Shanghai had a ball
With the whole Eighth Route Army last fall.
    She was screwed, with a smile,
    Seven times every mile,
The full length of the Chinese Great Wall.

81. OUTSPOKEN

A well-behaved woman named Pam
Once got in a terrible jam.
    When a fellow said, "Who
    Is the nation's best screw?"
She thoughtlessly answered, "I am."

8 2 . OH, HECK

There once was a Hollywood star
Whose breasts were the largest by far.
  No use copping a feel,
  For her bra is chrome-steel,
A habit men think quite bizarre.

8 3 . LOOKING GOOD

A bright fellow once met a young whore
Who wore nothing behind or before.
  He looked at her well,
  Said, "Whatever you sell,
I must say that I like the décor.'

8 4 . FAKE

Do you know why Joe seems to be furious?
He'd been treated in manner injurious.
  He was set for a lark
  With a girl in the dark,
And then found that her breastworks were spurious.

85. SPELLING

Deer hunting is greatest by far.
It's the one outdoor sport I don't bar.
    But that isn't puzzling.
    I like all that nuzzling,
Since I spell the word D-E-A-R.

86. UNSATISFACTORY

There was a young maid of Altoona,
Who said to an ardent young spooner,
    "It is simply no use,
    Put me down, turn me loose.
Though I come pretty soon, you come sooner."

87. WIGGLE THOSE FINGERS

There was a young fellow from Butte
Who married a girl who was mutte.
    "When she wants sex," he said,
    "And points to the bed,
The signs that she makes are so cutte."

88. NOT SO SMART

In a lane, a young fellow named Cooper
Committed a terrible blooper.
    He had his girl bare
    In his car, unaware
Of a vigilant nearby state trooper.

89. INGENUITY

A woman from old Monterey
Decided to try a new way.
    She got into bed
    And stood on her head
And found the men eager to pay.

90. BETTER THAN COMIC SONGS

An ebullient fellow named Marty,
A raucous lad, rather a smarty,
    Had screwed pretty Mabel
    Right there on the table,
And greatly enlivened the party.

9 1 . HOW'S THAT!

An experienced lecher, Stefan,
Keeps a woman upon a divan.
    Two more on a chair,
    All three of them bare
And keeps proving to them he's a man.

9 2 . NONCHALANT

A carefree young woman named Nola
At one time in a summer pergola
    Took care of three men
    Again and again
And did it on just Coca-Cola.

9 3 . A QUESTION OF MONEY

A little adultery spices
Our lives, but just look at those prices!
    If they charge all that dough,
    Men can't buy it, you know,
And there'll be a frustrational crisis.

9 4 . E N D U R A N C E

A soldier came back with the knack
Of enduring six hours in the sack.
  And without once withdrawing
  He'd keep up with his sawing—
So the ladies chipped in for a plaque.

9 5 . A G O O D S P O R T

Make a pass, if you will, at Miss Rogers.
You'll find she's not one of those dodgers.
  At the rooms that she rents
  All the joys are immense
As she sleeps with each one of the lodgers

9 6 . A L L T H E N E W S T H A T ' S F I T T O P R I N T

The *Times* tells the world what is doing;
Who's winning, who's losing, who's suing,
  Who's striking, who's stealing,
  Who's dying, who's healing,
But won't say a word on who's screwing.

97. IT'S THE FAULT OF
THE ROMANS

An astronomer said, "What's the use!
Our classical knowledge is loose.
    There can be nothing stupider
    Than to name that world Jupiter,
When we all know it should be called Zeus."

98. WHAT A HIDING PLACE!

There once was a genial old soul
Well known for the bank funds he stole.
    Although under suspicion,
    He defied extradition
From the depths of his mini-black hole.

99. PERFECT

The girl who is really unbeatable
Is the one with whom sex is repeatable;
    Who's eternally screwable
    And always renewable,
And who, most of all, is found eatable.

1 0 0 . GOOD ADVICE

Said a genial, self-confident chap,
To the pretty young thing on his lap,
    "Of course you can't leave.
    You're here to conceive,
And you'll love it, so don't be a sap."

1 0 1 . SCIENTIFIC ATTITUDE

There's a luscious young damsel, Celeste,
Who, everyone claims, is the best.
    But such secondhand views
    Only serve to confuse.
I prefer a more personal test.

1 0 2 . LOVING ONE'S WORK

When the men were all absent, Jane drooped,
And she liked it the best when they grouped.
    She worked them with vigor,
    Reducing their rigor,
And when done, felt delightfully pooped.

1 0 3 . SCRAPING THE BOTTOM OF THE BARREL

There was a young woman named Janey,
And no one alive is less brainy.
 In her search for a man
 She has gone to Iran
To wed Ayatollah Khomeini.

1 0 4 . A MATTER OF OPINION

There was a young woman named Chris,
Who said, when she squatted to piss,
 "Men aren't so bright,
 They do it upright,
When it's simpler to do it like this."

1 0 5 . MITIGATING CIRCUMSTANCES

A convinced Philistine named Delury
Had once slain a young poet in fury.
 The corpse, a wine-bibber,
 Had dealt in *vers libre*,
So Delury was thanked by the jury.

1 0 6 . D E S S E R T

There was a young woman named Rhoda
As sweet as a chocolate soda.
    It was such a delight
    To screw her at night
Then once more at dawn as a coda.

1 0 7 . T E M P T R E S S O F T H E N I L E

Cleopatra's a cute little minx
With a sex life that's loaded with kinks.
    Marcus A. she would steer amid
    The palms and Great Pyramid
And they'd screw on the head of the sphinx.

1 0 8 . W E A L L G E T O L D

There was an old lady of Brewster
Who would mutter, whenever I gewster,
    "You're losing the knack,
    Or you're missing the crack,
'Cause it don't feel as good as it yewster."

1 0 9 . SHE'S NO DOPE

Upon high Olympus, great Zeus
Muttered angrily, "Oh, what the deuce!
    It takes spiced ambrosia
    To get the nymphs cosier
And Hera supplies grapefruit juice."

1 1 0 . GOOD THINKING

There was a young lass of New York
Who loved fondling her boyfriend's big dork.
    She would stroke and embrace it,
    Then carefully place it
In the spot where her two thighs did fork.

1 1 1 . OH, DADDY!

A pious young minister's pappy
Had a sex life, diverse, hot, and snappy.
    It shocked his dear son
    When he had all that fun,
But it made girl parishioners happy.

1 1 2 . REAR VIEW

When a hardened old rake felt the twinge,
He'd go barreling off on a binge.
    His bawdy-house feats
    Involving girls' seats
Made the hardiest filles-de-joie cringe.

1 1 3 . APPAULING

Said a lighthearted girl from Salerno
"It is better to screw than to burn, oh."
    St. Paul soon took note
    Of this flagrant misquote,
And consigned her to Dante's Inferno.

1 1 4 . DECENCY ABOVE ALL

Julius Caesar would screw a fine quorum
Of girls in the old Roman forum.
    He made watchers pay,
    Or else turn away.
Thus conducting the show with decorum.

1 1 5 . I WON'T EVEN THINK ABOUT IT

A sweaty young yeti named Betty
Had a love in the park, Serengeti.
    An ungainly old gnu
    Who was faithful and true,
With love ready and heady and steady.

1 1 6 . UP IN THE AIR SO HIGH

A well-endowed lover named Walter
In charging his girl, did not falter,
    But he tripped on a stone
    And instantly shone
As a great (accidental) pole vaulter.

1 1 7 . STRAIGHT AS A DIE

A grave Church of England D. D.
Ran off with a nice chimpanzee.
    But do not feel remorse,
    She was female, of course.
The vicar's not queer, don't you see.

1 1 8 . WHAT ABOUT THAT IN BETWEEN

There was an old fellow named Murray,
Whose wife said, "My God, how I worry.
    When we're both in bed,
    He's either quite dead,
Or he's finished in much too much hurry."

1 1 9 . SELF-CONFIDENCE

A young wheeler-dealer named Timothy,
Said, "Why, all that I need is proximity.
    Just show me my prey and
    Then give me one day and
They'll be screwed with complete equanimity

1 2 0 . WHILE THE CAT'S AWAY

A doughty old knight of Belgrade
Cantered southward to join the Crusade.
    His lady, recalling
    That squires knew their balling,
Faced a husbandless life undismayed.

1 2 1 . WEAK SPOT

The Homeric young fighter Achilles
Was great with the fair Trojan fillies,
    But Paris said, "We'll
    Just aim at his heel."
Now Achilles is pushing up lilies.

1 2 2 . DON'T TAKE MY WORD FOR
I T

When they gave me a scroll as "the best,"
They just wrote those two words, but the rest
    You can call out en masse
    (Unless you're a lass
Who'd like putting the thing to the test).

1 2 3 . OOH, LA, LA

Parisian girls mutter "Peut-être"
Once they've earned their well-known scarlet lettre,
    So when told "Je t'adore"
    They answer, "Encore?
Well—provided monsieur does it bettre."

1 2 4 . AND IT'S SACRED, TOO

A Brahman who lives in Bombay
Shrieked with horror and fainted today,
    When he found that somehow
    He had buggered a cow.
(Her pleased "moo" was what gave it away.)

1 2 5 . COMPLICATIONS MAY SET IN

Sex need *not* be at all conversational.
Without talking, it's still inspirational.
    But mind you're not burned
    For many have learned
The act can be baby-creational.

1 2 6 . ANY PORT IN A STORM

A wily old shiek of Arabia
Said, "My eunuchs tell me that there may be a
    Great dearth of Circassians
    To surfeit my passions.
But my camel's here—labia are labia."

127. ALWAYS THE GENTLEMAN

I met a young lass named Roberta
And I did all I could to divert 'er.
    But talk wouldn't do.
    She wanted to screw.
I gave in. After all, could I hurt 'er?

128. CONNOISSEUR

When expecting erotic delight,
Make sure that the wine is just right.
    You should always have red
    With brunettes in your bed,
But with blondes, just be certain it's white.

129. WHAT MORE IS THERE?

There was a young woman named Ina
Who said, "There is nothing that's finer
    Then my good husband, Howie,
    Who's a real knockout zowie,
Whenever he's near my vagina."

1 3 0 . ENGLISH LOVE AT FIVE

"It is nice when a young lady *has* tea."
Said Jane, "though it may be just fast tea.
    These revels and spasms
    Of tealess orgasms
End up, I'm afraid, being nasty."

1 3 1 . EXPERIENCE LOVE AT ANY TIME

A gentleman shouldn't bring haste for it.
He must see that the lady is paced for it.
    He must kindle the fire,
    Raise it carefully higher,
Producing a connoisseur's taste for it.

1 3 2 . RANDOM POSITIONS

Said John, "In my recent attacking,
Variety seems to be lacking.
    Let's drop on the bed
    From the lamps overhead
And however we land, let's get cracking."

1 3 3 . MOTHER GOOSE REVISITED

They say Jack and his best girlfriend, Jill,
One nice day went and climbed up a hill.
　　Was it water they're after?
　　Then why all that laughter?
And how come Jill made sure of her pill?

1 3 4 . —AND REVISITED

Where is Little Boy Blue this fine morn?
In the haystack as sure as you're born.
　　But he isn't asleep;
　　He's with Little Bo-Peep;
And just look where he's putting his horn.

1 3 5 . —AND REVISITED

"As for screwing," said Little Miss Muffet,
"I proclaim here and how that I love it.
　　I defy the authority
　　of The Moral Majority.
They can take all their preaching and stuff it."

1 3 6 . — A N D   R E V I S I T E D

Jack Horner, they say, probed a pie
With his thumb, for a plum, but "Oh, my
    How the years will produce
    A much better-placed use
For his thumb," the young maidens all cry.

1 3 7 . — A N D   R E V I S I T E D

We treat Mary (of unknown locality)
And her lamb without proper formality.
    Let me ask: Do we view
    A young ram or a ewe?
Just pure love? Or a budding bestiality?

1 3 8 . M A R I T A L   A R G U M E N T ,   P A R T   O N E

It is sad when two loved ones fall out
Over things they should not fight about.
    They should stay sentimen-i-tal
    About all that is gen-i-tal
And make inches no object of doubt.

139. MARITAL ARGUMENT, PART TWO

Said the husband, with smiling urbanity,
"I possess penile superhumanity."
    Said his wife, "But the score
    Of his inches is four.
The rest of it's just his insanity."

140. MARITAL ARGUMENT, PART THREE

Hubby's fury then reached incandescence.
And he said, "My respect for her lessens,
    Because four is the *least*."
    "Not so, you vile beast;
That's its length in a state of tumescence."

141. MARITAL ARGUMENT, PART FOUR

"Four inches where *you* are concerned,
You old bag," said her man, really burned.
    "All your girls," she said, "gave it
    (In this signed affidavit)
As four!" and the court stands adjourned.

1 4 2 . DOWN WITH RACISM

An American fellow from Tucson
And a lady Korean from Pusan
    Made it sexually
    (Internationally)
And for that they deserve no abuse, son.

1 4 3 . CRIME AND PUNISHMENT

Please don't tell me that sex doesn't matter.
It will sometimes make ladies grow fatter.
    And then, don't you see,
    What was two becomes three,
With that nerve-racking sound—pitter, patter.

1 4 4 . HOPE ABANDONED

Said Mrs. Smith sadly, "J'accuse
Mr. Smith of what does not amuse.
    He will start things all right
    Any time of the night,
But then almost at once blows his fuse."

An Engrossment of Limericks
by John Ciardi

1 .

There once was a girl who intended
To keep herself morally splendid
    And ascend unto Glory,
    Which is not a bad story,
Except that that's not how it ended.

2 .

There once was a lady who thought
Only one thing, but thought it a lot.
    She thought yes and no,
    Till at eighty or so
She decided she rather thought not.

3.

Said a specialty hooker named Jean,
Who made the Jacuzzi her scene,
  "A rub-a-dub-dub,
  Three men in a tub
Not only come close—they come clean."

4.

A rather shy call girl named Sue
Cut slits in the covers she drew
  Up over her head
  When she got into bed—
Three marked "Service" and one "Peek-a-boo!"

5.

There were two consenting adults
Who agreed that they would not repulse
  One another's advances
  But just take their chances
And accept the result—or results.

6 .

At chit-chat last week with the duchess,
She remarked, "My dear boy, in as much as
    His Grace is away,
    And it's raining today,
What say we cut up a few touches?"

7 ·

An aged Rumanian whore
Taught her daughters the art and the lore
    Of keeping the house
    When shedding a spouse.
It beats peddling ass door to door.

8 .

"I had rather believed," said the earl,
"Room service would send up a girl.
    But we have gone this far.
    And, well, there you are.
And I say, let's give it a whirl."

9 .

There was a promoter named Hugh,
Who promoted a dance called The Screw.
    Disco by disco
    From New York to Frisco
He made it the in-thing to do.

1 0 .

There once was a fellow so vile
All our maids lost their heads for a while.
    Somehow what he lacked
    In breeding and tact
He made up for by sheer lack of style.

1 1 .

"It's your daughter," said Constable Fred.
"She's too flouncy by half. It's been said
    Every bitch has her day,
    But I'd rather not say
What that girl's taken into her head."

12.

There once was a farmer named Hicks,
Who used ewes for unusual tricks
    And went on at such length
    That he'd sapped all his strength
By the time he had turned ninety-six.

13.

One semester a young prof named Innis
Taught two hundred coeds what sin is.
    Not, bad, I acknowledge,
    For a small country college,
But not worth recording in Guinness.

14.

A pious young priest from South Bend
Prayed through long sleepless nights with a friend
    Till she started to swell.
    Then they saw all too well
Prayer can't change how it goes in the end.

1 5 .

Said an overfastidious gent
To a whore, "If you mean to give vent
    To my passions, I hope
    You've made good use of soap,
And have grown to the age of consent."

1 6 .

There was a young lodger named Byrd,
Who woke in the night. Had he heard
    Something stir? Was a hand
    Softly fondling his gland?
Yes, he had, and it was.—'Pon my word!

1 7 .

A Pavlovian student named Zell
Trained girls to respond to a bell
    By shedding their clothes
    And assuming the pose.
He claims that it works rather well.

18.

An ugly young fellow named Weems
Discovered a girl in his dreams.
    At very first sight
    She took such a fright
She woke him with blood-curdling screams.

19.

I can't tell you much about Slade.
He just came for a weekend and stayed,
    Making rather too free
    With my household and me,
And begetting four sons by our maid.

20.

There was a young man named Mahoney
Who was thought of, by some, as a phony.
    He did talk up a storm.
    But come time to perform
He sure had a lot of baloney.

2 1 .

A businesslike lady once baited
The door of her flat with X-rated
    Interior views,
      And, in neon, FREE BOOZE.
Then stretched out on a bearskin and waited.

2 2 .

An angry young fellow once wrote
His ex-girlfriend a rather firm note
    In such lurid detail
    It caught fire in the mail.
—Which leaves me unable to quote.

2 3 .

There once was a Jerry named Ford
Who suggested he might climb aboard
    The campaign express
    If asked, but I guess
The suggestion was largely ignored.

2 4 .

Jimmy Carter came on with a grin
All over his puss. To begin
    It seemed rather cute.
    But it's no substitute
For knowing what century you're in.

2 5 .

There once was a slicker named Dick,
Who, no matter how dirty the trick,
    Invoked the authority
    Of the silent majority
Till he found he could not make it stick.

2 6 .

There once was a widow named Jackie,
Whose wardrobe was getting plain tacky.
    So she married Ari
    And went to Paree
And near bought the town out, by cracky.

2 7 .

There once was an old pro named Spiro,
Who ran out on the field like a hero.
    And he sure was a slickjack
    At running a kickback,
But he fumbled, and now he's a zero.

2 8 .

A word spout named Howard Cosell
Set his sights on the language Nobel
    By overinflating
    His confabulating,
But to blow hard is not to blow well.

2 9 .

There once was a baker of parts
Who wasted no time on false starts.
    He turned out pies and cakes
    And fine bread in two shakes,
Leaving plenty of time for the tarts.

3 0 .

There was an old hornman who jammed
All night with two broads. When they scrammed
    An hour after dawn,
    He looked at his horn
And said, grinning, "Well, I'll be goddamned!"

3 1 .

There was a young lady from Queens,
Who while still in the blush of her teens
    Developed a range
    Of behavior so strange
It stirred rumors of recessive genes.

3 2 .

There was a young fellow who knew
Drinking, dicing, and whoring won't do.
    Which one might suppose
    Is plain fact, though, God knows,
Such knowledge is given to few.

33.

One evening a matron named Potter
Was debauched by a young squire who caught her
    In the depths of her garden.
    Having done, he begged pardon,
Saying, "Oops! I meant that for your daughter!"

34.

There was a young beauty named Mia,
Who never quite got the idea,
    Or who wasn't inclined
    To what boys have in mind.
Either way they stopped coming to see a.

35.

An eager young actress named Hartz
Let directors make free with her parts.
    What else can you do
    When you're just twenty-two
And not yet a name in the arts?

3 6 .

There was a young longhorn named Lew,
Whose card read, "Have doodle. Will do."
    But the best he could doodle
    Looked like a wet noodle
In a shoot-out with my sister Sue.

3 7 .

There was a young lady so nice
She wore rubber pants filled with ice
    Which kept her so cool
    She got halfway through school
With no need of sexual advice.

3 8 .

There was a young lady named Mame,
Whose parents believed it a shame
    To reject all the beaus
    Who came round to propose.
But she didn't. That's not why they came.

39.

Said Tiresias to Oedipus Rex,
"I'm too old to care about sex,
 But I'm telling you, brother,
 That queen's a mean mother
And she's setting you up for a hex."

40.

There was a pragmatic young SPAR
Who would not let the boys go too far.
 An orgasm or two,
 She believed, ought to do,
After which she'd say, "Well, there you are."

41.

There once was a cad from New Paltz
Who, among his less odious faults,
 Scorned romance as "red tape."
 He preferred simple rape
Without what he called "all that schmaltz."

42.

Said an underworked harlot from Kew
After lying all night between two
    Post-Edwardian beaus,
    "At Madame Tussaud's
Ah've seen sports what was livelier than you!"

43.

There's not much to be said for the style
Of the various lairds of Argyle.
    They just flip up the kilt
    And plunge to the hilt
In the lasses they choose to defile.

44.

In Shanghai a lady named Jinx
Got blind drunk on oddly mixed drinks.
    She awoke in a bunk
    In the hold of a junk
With no light but what passed through two Chinks.

45 .

My professor of sex claimed he knew
A hundred and one things to do.
    My girlfriend ain't much
    At book-learning, as such,
But she knows a hundred and two.

46 .

There was a teenager named Clem,
Who referred to all girls as "Oh—them."
    Then one night his dad
    Stopped to say "Good night, lad,"
And withdrew with, "Oh, well now—ahem!"

47 .

A sweetly developed young creature
Developed a crush on her teacher
    Who developed a lump
    That developed a bump
That is now her most prominent feature.

48.

There's no help for poor Freddy O'Day.
He felt dismal about being gay.
    Then a willing young bitch
    Tried to teach him to switch,
But he found it just ghastly that way.

49.

There was a young lady named Hammer
With a s-s-s-s—stammer.
    I had gone all the way
    Before she could say
She was dosed. Now I've got it, goddamn 'er!

50.

There was an old farmer named Swift,
Who went into town and got spiffed.
    He woke in a sty
    With a sow standing by
And said, "Now, dear, no use getting miffed!"

51.

Said Miss Atkins, "Young man, you're a bore!
I don't mind your smashing my door
    And just forging ahead
    Without a word said,
But why always here on the floor?"

52.

To St. Peter an ex-dean of Goucher
Declared she had let no man touch her.
    After careful review
    He let her pass through,
But he shrugged as he OK'd her voucher.

53.

A gifted old man from Darjeeling
Read sweet Susie's tea leaves, revealing
    The quite sordid facts
    Of various acts
The pious young fraud was concealing.

5 4 .

There was an old hooker named Ryan,
Who kept tryan and tryan and tryan.
    She tried all the way
    From Maine to L.A.,
But not even the Okies were byan.

5 5 .

On a survey of first dates Prof. Ness
Asked girls, "Would you care to undress?"
    He found 8-4-point-6
    Said, indignantly, "Nix!"
But that 1-5-point-4 answered "Yes!"

5 6 .

A pert little lady named Bobbie
Used to stroll through the Fontainebleu lobby
    Attracting the stares
    Of chance millionaires
Not entirely, I think, as a hobby.

176

5 7 .

There was a young tourist in Turin
For winin' and dinin' and whorin'.
    But the girls wouldn't do,
    The pasta was glue,
And the wine tasted vaguely of urine.

5 8 .

Said a porno queen, "Yes, I take care
To give everyone reason to stare.
    But the play of my parts
    Is all for the arts,
Or I just couldn't bear what I bare."

5 9 .

There was a young lady of Florence
Who could not abide D. H. Lawrence.
    When invited by Frieda
    To follow the leader
She expressed what is best called abhorrence.

60.

We don't know much of Phallos, the Greek.
He engaged seven sluts for a week.
    But the two who survived,
    Upon being revived,
Were too flabbergasted to speak.

61.

The once-esteemed Lady Hortense
Contracted from one of our gents
    A social bequest
    She passed on to the rest
With what we feel was malice prepense.

62.

There once was a girl who drank gin.
That isn't too bad to begin,
    But reiteration
    Shows a high correlation
With behavioral lapses called sin.

6 3 .

There was a young lady named Hope,
Whose Ma washed her mouth out with soap
    When she found her asprawl
    With three boys in the hall
And doing her utmost to cope.

6 4 .

There once was a starving old poet
Who never could sell what he wroet.
    He practiced austerity
    For the sake of posterity,
But he left it not even one quoet.

6 5 .

An Annapolis madam named Gideon
Used to say on inviting a middy in,
    "Now, lad, don't be nervous.
    It gets hard in the service,
But my girls all have soft tums to tiddy in."

66.

A young do-it-yourselfer once screwed
Two pieces together. If you'd
    Like to know what he made,
    You must ask Adelaide
And her little kid sister, Gertrude.

67.

At our last dance a young man named Schacht
Was admired by the girls for his tact.
    When he wanted a lay
    He would bow low and say,
"May I have your next sexual act?"

68.

A young physicist working for Myles
Left a couple of lead-covered vials
    On the seat of his chair.
    When he got up from there
He had an-atomic-al piles.

6 9 .

I've a theory I'd like to propound.
It was not, as some scholars have found,
   The apple aglow
   On the tree that brought woe
To the world, but that pair on the ground.

7 0 .

The old woman who lived in a shoe,
When she had nothing better to do,
   Would bed down her dears
   After boxing their ears,
And relax with a cobbler or two.

7 1 .

There once was a farmer named Jives,
Who grew tired of his seven old wives.
   He gave each as her pittance
   Some cats and some kittens
And herded them out of St. Ives.

7 2 .

To his bride whispered J. Osgood Neely,
"My dear, let us love so ideally
  That nothing so crude
  As sex need intrude
On our Eden." Said she, "You mean—really?"

7 3 .

The groom woke up late the third day
To discover his bride's best friend, Mae,
  Had come for a visit,
  And crying, "Where is it?"
Was tearing the bedclothes away.

7 4 .

There was a young fellow on Bimini
Who chartered a yacht for three women he
  Intended to trick.
  But the swells made him sick.
An ambitious young cad, but no seaman he.

7 5 .

An ambitious young fellow named Knight
Ended up on Skid Row. He got tight,
    And rolled in foul ditches
    With badly poxed bitches.
And now he has no end in sight.

7 6 .

There once was a young farmer's daughter
Who learned a bit late that she oughter
    Have studied what teacher,
    Her mom, and the preacher
Believed they had already taught her.

7 7 .

Life is merry in old Monterey.
When the duke woke up frisky today
    And had at her Grace,
    She kept doubling the pace
While the chambermaids shouted "Olé!"

7 8 .

There was an old geezer named Blair,
Who used to get girls to strip bare
    By slipping red ants
    In their bras and their pants.
Yes, it works—but it lacks *savoir-faire*.

7 9 .

In Vegas a hooker named Lou
Ran a number with one gent, then two.
    When a third asked to play
    She said, "Well, OK.
But that does it. *Rien ne vas plus*.

8 0 .

Over beer in a dimly lit bar
I was puffing a ten-cent cigar,
    When a girl of a sort
    Said, "You look like a sport."
And my wife, in the shadows, said, "Ha!"

8 1 .

Said Romeo climbing the fence,
"I love you, but this makes no sense.
    That damned wire has ripped
    My left ball and snipped
Both my prepuce and vas deferens."

8 2 .

"Shall we?" said Fred pinching Flo,
"Or are you as pure as the snow?"
    "That's two questions," said she,
    "And my answer must be
—If you've got fifty bucks—yes and no."

8 3 .

A writer has got to be deft.
When he finds he has no money left,
    Can he do without meals?
    To hell with ideals.
Learn to toss off a *roman à cleft*.

8 4 .

A raffiné poet named Potz
Took a rather high view of the otz.
    He was quick to proclaim
    His hard gemlike flame,
But the best he could manage was quotz.

8 5 .

There was a young husband named Dan,
Who set up his wife in a van
    And sent her to park
    Behind bars after dark.
It is hard to think well of that man.

8 6 .

Imprudent and unwed Mae-Bette
Had to shop for a basic layette.
    When they told her the price
    She gasped once or twice,
But she paid. And has more to pay yet.

8 7 .

A mechanic who married a shrew
Got her tamed in a minute or two.
    He just took out his kit
    And fiddled a bit.
All it took was a turn of the screw.

8 8 .

At the orgy last night Dionysus
In a rather remarkable nisus
    Had ten maids, a goat,
    Four pink boys, and a shoat
In sixteen consecutive trices.

8 9 .

There once was a wife who was sure
She was right. And she was. Till a whore
    Who was glad to be wrong
    Sang the old boy a song,
And they ran off to Cannes. *Vive l'amour!*

90.

There was a young dumpling from Boulder
Who loved to ride dear daddy's shoulder.
    Dad, at first, thought it fun.
    Then she turned twenty-one,
And he thought she should know—so he told her.

91.

There once was a cocky Eurasian
Who kept rising to every occasion.
    From what I have heard,
    When nothing occurred
He still rose, by sheer self-persuasion.

92.

A learned and truly exquisite
Young miss paid her tutor a visit.
    When, testing her thesis,
    He suggested syncresis,
She responded, in form, "*Vidilicet.*"

9 3 ·

There was a young man from St. Kitt's
With an itch that was giving him fits.
  It seems that a peach
  He picked up on the beach
Had left his bed full of strange nits.

9 4 ·

On the ski slopes young Dr. MacPrutt
Hit an ice slick and lit on his butt
  On a jagged rock shelf
  Thus divesting himself
Of what laymen would call his left nut.

9 5 ·

A gracious young hostess named Ewing
Believed she had only been doing
  Her ladylike best
  To welcome a guest,
And was startled when he called it "screwing."

9 6 .

A meticulous young dean named Lester
Took a girl to his rooms and undressed her.
    Then took out some charts
    And compared all her parts
With the norms for the current semester.

9 7 .

There was an old miser of whom
Little good could be said. I presume
    His cash did him credit.
    But, though no one said it,
He stank like the dungheap of Doom.

9 8 .

A puny Greek stripling named Kimon
Turned into a sexual demon
    After praying to Hera
    For various sera
Compounded of powdered goat semen.

99.

I suppose it did seem indiscrete
Of Myra to dance down the street
    With her all on display.
    Yet, at bottom, I'd say
The impulse was really quite sweet.

100.

A chap who was sailing for Singapore
Left room in his seabag to bring a whore
    Then forgot that he had
    Until she turned bad,
Which tended to make the whole thing a bore.

101.

A proper young miss who got stewed
Awoke rather shockingly nude
    In a room with six gents
    And a terrified sense
That she had been—and was being—screwed.

1 0 2 .

There was a young man who give chase
To loose women—a pitiful case
    Made more sordid by wine,
    Till, at seventy-nine,
He died with an evil grimace.

1 0 3 .

South of Nome there's a farmer I know
Whose fields are all covered with snow
    From September to May
    When the stuff melts away
Leaving just time for nothing to grow.

1 0 4 .

At the last dance a scoundrel from Media
Picked a wallflower and whispered, "I needia!"
    Said the maiden undaunted,
    It's nice to be wanted,
But you could have been just a bit speedia."

1 0 5 .

In the north woods a girl from St. Jacques
Was willing to give it a crack.
  But her boyfriend, young Fred,
  Kept pushing ahead
And circling to sneak up in back.

1 0 6 .

Said a busy young Texan in Rome,
Who had bought up the Vatican dome,
  "It's not just for the art,
  Though I'd say that's right smart,
It's the challenge of getting it home."

1 0 7 .

There was a young lady from Ipswich
Who grew famous for making her hips twitch
  While shedding her clothes
  Which, as one might suppose,
Were held on by no more than a slip stitch.

1 0 8 .

I won't say the girls at St. Francis
Intend to encourage lewd glances,
 But can one believe
 They are merely naïve
When they come in the nude to school dances?

1 0 9 .

There was an old salt on the Banks
Who said to a mermaid, "No thanks.
 The last time I tried
 Those scales took my hide
Clear off from my crotch to my shanks."

1 1 0 .

An elegant lady named Pruitt
Did not absolutely eschew it
 But demanded such bowing
 And scraping and vowing
That most gents walked out saying, "Screw it!"

1 1 1 .

Our German prof, Doktor von Strüss,
Is not one to play fast and loose,
    But at faculty do's,
    Having sampled the booze,
He's been known to try out a sly goose.

1 1 2 .

Said a Washington hostess named Moll
To a subclerk she passed in the hall,
    "Once his Excellency goes,
    I should like to propose
That we not stand on strict protocol."

1 1 3 .

At the Last Chance Saloon good old Mabel
Used to put all her cards on the table,
    And herself on request.
    If she wasn't the best,
She was open, aboveboard, and able.

1 1 4 .

Said a well-preserved harlot named Gwen,
"I have chalked up my three score and ten.
    I can't ask for much more,
    But I'm going for four,
And maybe I'll stop scoring then."

1 1 5 .

A well-heeled old dame named Roberta
Had been brought up to think sex would hurta.
    But she found, in the main,
    A high threshhold of pain
Was an asset that would not deserta.

1 1 6 .

There was a young lady from Butte
Who acted a little too cute,
    Especially for
    A five-dollar whore
In a house that lacked even repute.

117.

There was a young man from Green Bay
Who awoke with a sense of dismay
    To find in his bed
    A girl who had read
All of Edna St. Vincent Millay.

118.

At the Ritz a young lady drank lunch
With a roué who ordered rum punch.
    As they clinked cup to cup
    He said, "Well, bottom's up!"
—Which I'd say was a rather shrewd hunch.

119.

There was a young lady from Deanstown
Who would have walked off with the queen's crown
    At the CYO rally
    Had not Father O'Malley
Caught her playing boy-girl with her jeans down.

1 2 0 .

There was an old hooker who blew.
What I mean is, she left town. If you
    Understood what I said
    To mean she gave head,
Well, I guess there was some of that, too.

1 2 1 .

Said a fair-skinned young lady named Nan
As she stretched on the beach, "I won't tan.
    Moonbeams are too thin
    To damage my skin
When I cover myself with a man."

1 2 2 .

Herr General von und zum Hallus
Had a caisson attached to his phallus,
    And would ride into battle
    With his brass balls a-rattle
While singing "Deutschland Über Alles!"

1 2 3 .

At fair time Miz Flowerie-Belle Lee
Takes in city gents for a fee.
  But she lets us homefolk
  Perch up in that oak
By her winder and watch the show—free.

1 2 4 .

Have you heard about poor Angelique?
She canoed up the river last week
  With some damn lumberjack.
  And though they came back,
We're afraid she's been left up the creek.

1 2 5 .

There was a young lady named Lassiter,
Whose permission could not have been taciter.
  She would lie on the lawn
  Barely stifling a yawn
While our lads stood in line for a pass at her.

1 2 6 .

When he rode out the old laird of Clyde
Used to make it a matter of pride
    To scoop up a lass,
    Have a quick piece of ass,
And discard her without breaking stride.

1 2 7 .

There was a young lady named Jansen,
Whose Ma said, "I don't mind romancin'.
    You're young. Have your fling.
    But remember one thing:
When you stay out all night, keep on dancin'."

1 2 8 .

The first troops under Spanish command
To set foot on Floridian sand
    Found a Seminole maid
    Who took trinkets in trade
And gave them the lay of the land.

129.

An expert mechanic named Nims
Kept a full range of foam-rubber shims
    For adjusting the set
    Of young ladies he'd get
To indulge his meticulous whims.

130.

There was a young widow named Gormley,
Who approached a young man quite inform'ly
    And asked to be screwed.
    "Please do not think me rude,"
She explained, "I do not do this norm'ly."

131.

There once was an artist who drew
Large crowds to blank canvases. "Ooh!"
    Cried the critics, "the essence
    Of the post-incandescence
Of conceptualized déjà vu!"

132.

> An expensive young harlot named Ann
> Just can't bear to say no to a man.
>> So for five bucks a week
>> She allows us a peek
> On what she calls her lay-away plan.

133.

> There was a young person named Clarence,
> Who cabled from Sweden: "Dear Parents:
>> Sex-change operation
>> Creates new relation.
> As Clara, implore your forebearance."

134.

> There once was a girl from Piscataway
> Who said to a school chum, "Is that a way
>> To treat an old friend?
>> You've got the wrong end.
> Stop it, please. I do not like this thataway."

135.

A middle-aged lady once reckoned
The passage of time to a second,
        Then rounded it out
        To ten years—just about—
Since the last man had come when she beckoned.

136.

There once was a nervous young Finn
Who had barely begun to get in
        To a lady he knew
        When her husband said "Boo!"
—And he damned near jumped out of her skin.

137.

There was a young man who drank rum.
In time he became a rank bum
        And his morals regressed.
        I have tried the same test
And I have to confess mine shrank some.

1 3 8 .

An impoverished young couple named Skeat
Used to bundle to save on the heat.
    But six kids in five years
    Left them in such arrears
They have never again made ends meet.

1 3 9 .

One day when a lady named Anne
Went up to the sun roof to tan
    A gent in a copter
    Flew over and dropped her
Some ads for a crash-diet plan.

1 4 0 .

Please take note of the ex Mrs. Tolliver.
Her husband tried making a doll of her.
    She did learn to blink,
    And say Papa, and wink.
But she found that did not express all of her.

204

141.

At a gay bar two young men inspected
Some girls whom they promptly rejected
      In blank ennui.
      It was easy to see
They were totally other-directed.

142.

There was a young lady named Kate,
Who found she was putting on weight.
      She requested a diet.
      Said her doctor, "Sure. Try it.
But your intake is more than you ate."

143.

Here's a toast to my old sweetheart Sal,
A real down-home old-fashioned gal.
      For though once or twice
      She was busted for vice,
To me she was always a pal.

144.

What Asimov lacks of pure style
He makes up for—well, once in a while—
    By the way he can bluster
    From the depths of lackluster
To the (almost) transcendently vile.